A New

Dick B.'s Reference Titles on Alcoholics Anonymous History
Paradise Research Publications, Inc., Publisher;
Good Book Publishing Company, Distributor P.O. Box 837, Kihei, HI 96753-0837
Phone/Fax: (808) 874 4876; Email: dickb@dickb.com; URL: http://www.dickb.com/index.shtml

Publisher's June 1, 2006 List of Titles by Author Dick B.

A New Way Out
Anne Smith's Journal, 1933-1939
By the Power of God: A Guide to Early A.A. Groups & Forming Similar Groups Today
Cured!: Proven Help for Alcoholics and Addicts
Dr. Bob and His Library
God and Alcoholism: Our Growing Opportunity in the 21st Century
Good Morning!: Quiet Time, Morning Watch, Meditation, and Early A.A.
Henrietta B. Seiberling: Ohio's Lady with a Cause
Making Known The Biblical History and Roots of Alcoholics Anonymous: A 16-Year Research, Writing, Publishing and Fact Dissemination Project
New Light on Alcoholism: God, Sam Shoemaker, and A.A.
The Akron Genesis of Alcoholics Anonymous
The Books Early AAs Read for Spiritual Growth
The Conversion of Bill W.
The First Nationwide A.A. History Conference - Comments of Dick B.
The Golden Text of A.A.: God, the Pioneers, and Real Spirituality
The Good Book and The Big Book: A.A.'s Roots in the Bible
The Good Book-Big Book Guidebook
The James Club: The Original A.A. Program's Absolute Essentials
The Oxford Group & Alcoholics Anonymous
That Amazing Grace (Clarence & Grace S.)
Turning Point: A History of Early A.A.'s Spiritual Roots and Successes
Twelve Steps for You: Let Our Creator, A.A. History, and the Big Book Be Your Guide
Utilizing Early A.A.'s Spiritual Roots for Recovery Today
When Early AA s Were Cured and Why
Why Early A.A. Succeeded: The Good Book in Alcoholics Anonymous Yesterday and Today (a Bible Study Primer)

Available through other distributors

Hope: The Story of Geraldine O. Delaney, 2d ed. (Alina Lodge)
Our Faith Community A.A. Legacy (Dick B., Editor and compiler)
(Came to Believe Publications)
Courage to Change (with Bill Pittman) (Hazelden)
Women Pioneers of AA (Dick B., contributor) (Hazelden)

A New Way In

Reaching the Heart of a Child of God in Recovery with His Own, Powerful, Historical Roots

Dick B.

Paradise Research Publications, Inc.
Kihei, Maui, Hawaii

Paradise Research Publications, Inc.
PO Box 837
Kihci, HI 96753-0837
(808 874 4876)
Email: dickb@dickb.com
URL: http://www.dickb.com/index.shtml

Printed in the United States of America

Cover Design by American Creations of Maui

This Paradise Research Publications Edition is published by arrangement with Good Book Publishing Company, PO Box 837, Kihei, HI: 96753-0837

Note: All Bible verses quoted in this book, unless otherwise noted, are from the Authorized (or "King James") Version. The letters "KJV" are used when necessary to distinguish it from other versions.

ISBN 1-885803-88-5

Contents

Part 1

The Akron A.A. Christian Program That Cured Alcoholics

Beginning with 1934, A.A. Co-founder Bill Wilson said many times that he was unable to get a single person sober in the six months that he scurried from Towns Hospital to Calvary Rescue Mission to Oxford Group meetings in New York. Bill feverishly chased drunks, but not one of them got sober. Furthermore, as Bill began bringing drunks to the home that he and Lois Wilson shared, the result was the same for several years. Not one person got sober. And even in the earliest years of New York A.A., the best Wilson could claim was that his partner Hank Parkhurst got sober—only to drink at a later point; and that John Henry Fitzhugh Mayo—son of an Episcopal minister—was the other newcomer who was reached successfully by Bill.

Let's therefore begin with, and focus on, the Akron program of 1935 to 1938, that Bill and Co-founder Dr. Bob developed *together*. This was the program that, by 1937, had produced forty alcoholic recoveries among men with two years or less of continuous sobriety. Counting noses, Bill and Bob found they had a total success record of 50% among these men, with a further, additional 25% success record among pioneers who relapsed but returned to sobriety.

The Frank Amos Written Summary of the Pioneer Program

The Early AAs' solution to their problems was reliance on the Creator. That reliance produced a documented 75% success rate in Akron, and very soon a 93% success rate in Cleveland among the medically incurable alcoholics who really tried. It's a story worth learning. It is simple. The approach was effective. And, because it worked, it attracted thousands to A.A. over the ensuing years. Medical cures and percentages of cure are what attract patients. Medical failures do not.

Fortunately, we still have a precise and accurate study of the Akron program that succeeded. Details that can be used this very day.

Bill Wilson had come to John D. Rockefeller, Jr., looking for money. Bill told the famous businessman the results Dr. Bob and his helpers were achieving in Akron. And Rockefeller decided to see for himself. He sent his agent Frank Amos out to Akron to investigate, and Amos reported back in two different papers exactly what he found. Amos had spent about a week in Akron, interviewed Dr. Bob and members of his fellowship, interviewed their wives, interviewed an Akron judge, an Akron attorney, medical colleagues, and others. And the following is the essence of the program, as Amos described it to Rockefeller:

- An alcoholic must realize that he is an alcoholic, incurable from a medical viewpoint, and that he must never drink anything with alcohol in it.
- He must surrender himself absolutely to God, realizing that in himself there is no hope.
- Not only must he want to stop drinking permanently, he must remove from his life other sins such as hatred, adultery, and others which frequently accompany alcoholism. Unless he will do this absolutely, Smith and his associates refuse to work with him.
- He must have devotions every morning–a "quiet time" of prayer and some reading from the Bible and other religious literature. Unless this is faithfully followed, there is grave danger of backsliding.
- He must be willing to help other alcoholics get straightened out. This throws up a protective barrier and strengthens his own willpower and convictions.
- It is important, but not vital, that he meet frequently with other reformed alcoholics and form both a social and a religious comradeship.
- Important, but not vital, that he attend some religious service at least once weekly.

Seven points, the last two—religious comradeship and church attendance—were simply *recommended*, but not required. The foregoing original A.A. program in Akron had no steps—twelve, six, or otherwise. It had no basic text but the Bible. For reading matter, it did circulate among the early fellowship members a large number of Christian books, devotionals, and articles. And you can read for yourself the foregoing detailed description of their program in *DR. BOB and the Good Oldtimers* (New York, NY: Alcoholics Anonymous World Services, Inc., 1980), pp. 130-36,

But the Frank Amos reports merely summarized the requirements of the program. Amos did not describe its activities with any particularity, and they need to be examined more fully. Though accurate as set forth, the importance of the original requirements and practices is not clear without a description of several additional points Amos didn't cover. Therefore, we've reconstructed from historical research a picture of the entire spiritual program of recovery developed in Akron between 1935 and 1938, and we've included the details summarized by Frank Amos.

The Specifics of What the Pioneers Did in Akron

They located a "real" alcoholic who needed help, wanted help, and would do whatever was expected of him: In the case of the first three AAs—Bill Wilson, Dr. Bob Smith, and Bill Dotson—someone had actually gone searching for each of the three as a "pigeon" needing help. Later, wives and relatives would sometimes bring a new man to Dr. Bob for help. Sometimes drunks appeared on the scene and asked for help. But searching out and "qualifying" the new person as one who was serious and willing was a critical part of the new program. He was interrogated to verify these points. And that very outreach itself contributed mightily to the success of the searchers.

They usually hospitalized the newcomer for about seven days: Hospitalization and/or medical help for a brief period was virtually a "must" for almost all the early A A members. Then, as now, there was danger of seizures, severe shaking, injury to self, and disorientation. Medical monitoring was considered prudent. During that period, only a Bible was allowed in the hospital room. Medications were administered. There were daily visits and lengthy talks by Dr. Bob with each patient. There were regular visits by recovered pioneers who apprised the newcomer of their own stories and successes. Just prior to discharge, there was a visit to the newcomer by Dr. Bob. He may have covered additional points about alcoholism, such as they were known at that time. But, primarily, he asked the new person to acknowledge his belief in the Creator. If there was an affirmative answer, Dr. Bob required the patient to make a "surrender" to Christ on his knees and join Dr. Bob in a prayer. And then there was release from the hospital.

They often offered food, shelter, and support in the home of some pioneer family. The two homes that first come to mind are those of Dr. Bob and his wife Anne Smith, and Wally G. and his wife Annabelle. In a sense, these live-in arrangements represented the first "half-way" houses as they are often called today. Recovery work in Akron did not begin or take place in groups or meetings or treatment centers; nor in rehabs or therapy or confinement. It took place primarily in homes, and that, in itself, constituted a very different situation from the program of the Oxford Group where Bill Wilson had previously cut his teeth in the New York area. As stated, Akron pioneer efforts took place primarily in the homes of people like Dr. Bob and Anne Smith. And in these homes, there were: (1) Daily get-togethers. (2) Bible studies and the reading of Christian literature and devotionals circulated by Dr. Bob and his wife. (3) Quiet times held by each individual who prayed, studied the Bible, and sought God's guidance. (4) Morning quiet time meetings led by Dr. Bob's wife for AAs and their families who listened to Anne teach from the Bible, prayed together, heard Anne share from her spiritual journal, discussed its contents with those present, and then sought guidance from God for the day. (5) Residents frequently discussed problems and Biblical solutions with Dr. Bob, Henrietta Seiberling, T. Henry Williams, and Anne Smith. And those who stayed over many days and nights in this or that home, broke bread, lived, and fellowshipped together. (6) Once a week the pioneers held a "regular" Wednesday meeting with "real" surrenders upstairs after the manner of James: 5:15-16. (7) Pioneers utilized a few of some twenty-eight Oxford Group life-changing practices such as Inventory, Confession, Conviction, and Restitution. (8) They then arranged visits to newcomers at the hospital. (9) They recommended church attendance by most. (10) They enjoyed social, religious, and family fellowship. (11) And it all began again.

There was one "Regular" meeting on Wednesdays at the home of T. Henry and Clarace Williams in Akron. Though it originally began as an Oxford Group meeting, it was not conducted like most Oxford Group meetings. Its members--Oxford Groupers, alcoholics, wives and children—were there to help alcoholics get well by spiritual means. Host T. Henry therefore called the meeting a "clandestine lodge" of the Oxford Group because it differed so much from the movement Frank Buchman and Sam Shoemaker were leading. Also, before the Wednesday meeting, leaders such as Dr. Bob, Anne, Henrietta Seiberling, and Mr. and Mrs. Williams would hold a Monday "setup" meeting where God's guidance was sought as to who should lead the Wednesday meeting and what its topic should be. On Wednesdays, there were none of the conventional Oxford Group testimonials nor were there any of what have today become alcoholic drunkalogs. The regular meeting opened with a prayer. Scripture was read, then group prayer, and then a brief group guidance circle. The meeting discussed a selected topic—whether from the Bible, a devotional, or a subject involving living by Biblical principles. The discussion was led by someone such as Dr. Bob, Henrietta Seiberling, or T. Henry Williams. There was intense focus on the study and discussion of the Bible's Book of James, Sermon on the Mount, and 1 Corinthians 13. There was a special time for "real" surrenders upstairs for the newcomers. Following those, arrangements were made downstairs for some in the group to visit newcomers at the Akron City Hospital. The meeting closed with the Lord's Prayer; socializing; and the exchange of Christian literature displayed on tables for the taking. There had been no drunkalogs. No Steps. No Big Book. No texts at all. Just the Bible and devotionals like *The Upper Room* and the specially valued lessons taught from James, Corinthians, and Matthew.

"Real Surrenders" to Christ, several Oxford Group practices, counseling with the Smiths and Henrietta Seiberling, study of Christian literature, and church attendance. (1) In order to belong to the Akron fellowship, newcomers had to make a "real surrender." This was akin to the altar call at rescue missions or confession of Christ with other believers in churches, except that it was a very small, private, action taken upstairs and away from the regular meeting. Four A.A. old-timers (Ed Andy, J. D. Holmes, Clarence Snyder, and Larry Bauer) have all verified orally and in writing that the Akron surrenders required acceptance of Jesus Christ as Lord and Saviour. They took place at the regular Wednesday meeting upstairs in the manner described in James 5:15-16. Kneeling, with "elders" at his side, the newcomer accepted Christ and, with the prayer partners, asked God to take alcohol out of his life and to help, guide, and strengthen him to live by cardinal Christian teachings such as those in the Four Absolutes—Honesty, Purity, Unselfishness, and Love. (2) Not so clear as to Akron is just how many of its pioneers completed such Oxford Group life-changing practices as Inventory, Confession, Conviction, and Restitution though there is mention of some. (3) Many men and women received counseling from Bob and Anne Smith, Henrietta Seiberling, and T. Henry Williams. They frequently studied or listened to Scripture, prayed, and discussed practical matters like jobs and family difficulties. Anne Smith worked extensively with new people and their families and formed a Woman's Group in Akron in A.A.'s second year. (4) A wide variety of Christian literature on the Bible, prayer, healing, love, the life of Christ, Shoemaker's writings, Oxford Group books, and daily study topics was passed around the fellowship and read by alcoholics and family members alike. (5) Though A.A. literature is devoid of significant mention of church, the Amos reports disclose that attendance at a church of one's choice was recommended. There is particular evidence that Roman Catholics were in touch with their own priests, and that the leaders—Bob, Anne, Henrietta, and Mr. and Mrs. Williams—all attended church.

Quiet Times: (held by individuals, by the group, and by the early birds in the morning with Anne Smith). The first condition of receiving revelation is *not* "listening" to God. The first condition of effective communication with the Creator is the establishment of one's standing as a child of God by accepting Jesus Christ as Lord and Saviour. With that accomplished, the new Christian is a member of the body of Christ, able to communicate with God and His son, and endowed with the ability to understand spiritual matters the "natural man" cannot comprehend. Hence, this was a vital part of the Akron programBevidenced by the "surrender" at the hospital and certainly the "real surrender" in the homes. Then, for born-again believers, quiet time consisted of reading the Bible, prayer to and seeking revelation from God, use of devotionals like *The Upper Room*, utilizing Anne Smith's Journal for teaching and instruction, and reading Christian literature such as Henry Drummond's *The Greatest Thing in the World,* Nora Smith Holm's *The Runner's Bible, The Upper Room,* and various studies of the Sermon on the Mount by Oswald Chambers, Glenn Clark, Emmet Fox, and E. Stanley Jones.

Intensive personal work with newcomers: Dr. Bob was called the "Prince of Twelfth Steppers" and worked personally with over 5000 alcoholics. Visits with newcomers by those who had already made the grade were a regular occurrence in Akron. And, though Bill's personal outreach efforts yielded little fruit when compared to the results in Akron, Bill Wilson was the original, vigorous hustler—seeking out new people at Oxford Group meetings, Towns Hospital, and Calvary Rescue Mission. However, the unquestioned, liveliest individual 12 Stepper was probably young Clarence H. Snyder. Before he formed the Cleveland group, Clarence was bringing alcoholics down to Akron on a regular basis. In Cleveland, Clarence was a dynamo seeking out drunks, taking them through Step classes, and getting new groups going. Cleveland groups grew from one to thirty in a year. And Clarence sponsored hundreds through the years—finally as the A.A. with the longest period of sobriety.

Self-government, self-decisions, and self-support within membership groups: Both Dr. Bob and Bill were raised in the tradition of the New England Congregational denominations. This meant that each church was governed by its members. It was supported by its members. And it was accountable to no higher power, official, office, or administration than the rule and vote of its own congregation. Whatever the way by which this concept reached A.A., this system became the rule for local A.A. groups though Dr. Bob was undeniably the "leader" in Akron in the early pioneer days. At the same time, Bob was always opposed to transferring control of the A.A. fellowship to New York.

Helping wives and families. Early AAs were male. Yet the earliest A. A. meetings in Akron were family affairs. Alkies, their wives, and their children would attend the meetings at the home of T. Henry and Clarace Williams. Oxford Group activists did the same. Henrietta Seiberling made sure all her children attended some of the meetings. The Smith kids attended many. Wives of members worked shoulder-to-shoulder with their husbands. Thus the work of T. Henry had the help of his wife Clarace. The work of Dr. Bob, that of Anne. The work of Wally G., that of his wife Annabelle. The work of Tom Lucas, that of his wife. And the work of Clarence Snyder, that of his wife Dorothy. But there were special needs of wives of alcoholics that began to be recognized right away. Anne Smith was at the head of the pack in meeting them. Throughout early A.A. stories, you find remarks that Anne was legendary with newcomers, that she was especially kind to wives, that as early as 1936, she formed a women's group, and that she was particularly helpful to Lois Wilson time and time again. Her crown jewel, of course, is *Anne Smith's Journal, 1933-1939*, which she wrote and used for teaching during all of A.A.'s formative years. It is filled with materials as suitable for dealing with the problems of family as with the alcoholic himself. Yet it's rarely mentioned even by A.A. historians, and never in A.A. literature itself. It's not my purpose to deal with women's issues or rights, or the absence of women as members of the earliest A.A. But it is quite clear that Anne Smith, Bob, Bill to some extent, and Lois later realized that the special problems of what some now call "the family disease" of alcoholism needed to be addressed, both for the sake of individuals, of those who suffer, and for A.A. itself. Even Lois Wilson huddled in New York with her little "kitchen group" for quite some time before the seeds of Al-Anon and its Family Groups began to appear and take root.

The Emphasis of Bob and Bill together: I have several times quoted or summarized the statements of Bob and Bill together on the platform of the Shrine Auditorium in Los Angeles in 1948. Their remarks were reported on page 17 of the Friday, March 26, 1948, issue of *The Tidings*. About 4,500 AAs and their families were present. Bill spoke about the importance of Divine Aid, the religious element in A.A., and prayer. Dr. Bob spoke about the importance of cultivating the habit of prayer and reading the Bible. Both men were warmly receivedBa testimony to their harmonious accord, consistency, and simplicity of presentation when appearing together. The event signaled the unanimity of intent, if not of experience and knowledge, between Bill and Bob.

Diversions from Akron's Program Called the Word-of-Mouth "Six Steps"

Set forth above are the seven points of the original A.A. program, as Frank Amos summarized them after careful investigation. Set forth too are quite detailed descriptions of exactly how AAs conducted their program—in terms of structure, hospitalization, work with newcomers, Bible study, prayer, reading of literature, utilization of some Oxford Group ideas, utilization of devotionals, utilization of Anne Smith's Journal, utilization of the Four Absolutes, confession of Christ, reliance on the Creator, obedience to God's will, and cleansing sin from one's conduct.

Dr. Bob said several times that he didn't write the 12 Steps and had nothing to do with writing them. He said their basic ideas came from A.A.'s study of and effort in the Bible. He said the Book of James, Jesus's Sermon on the Mount, and 1 Corinthians 13 were absolutely essential to the program. And he specifically said that, when A.A. began, there were no Steps; there were no traditions; and that the stories (drunkalogs) didn't amount to much. So far, then, we've provided an almost complete composite of what early AAs did, developed, and accomplished from their founding on June 10, 1935 through the publication of their Big Book in the Spring of 1939.

But there were curious sideshows—call them "diversions"—that seemed to accompany or follow the first years of the Akron program. Bill claimed there were six "word of mouth" elements being used for recovery. Yet there is no mention of them by Frank Amos or by Dr. Bob. Secondly, as Bill went in to a deep depression in the 1940's and 1950's, Dr. Bob seemed concerned that the principles and practices of early A.A.—principles and practices that were to have been made the subject of the original basic text—be made available in very simple form. And so it was that four Akron AA pamphlets emerged; and the pamphlets far more resembled the Frank Amos program than Bill's "six" word-of-mouth ideas or the elements of the Twelve Steps he wrote in the Big Book.

For a long time in my research, I kept hearing that there had been six steps before there were Twelve. In one way or another, Bill Wilson suggested this. In another way, Lois Wilson suggested it by quoting "six" Oxford Group tenets—tenets which very clearly did not exist in the history or annals of the Oxford Group. My tendency, therefore, was to point to these facts and reject Bill's "six" steps as bogus.

But I nonetheless encountered them in several different ways, phrased in several different forms, and emanating from several different alleged sources. The first phraseology appeared on a piece of paper handed to me in New York by Bill's secretary, Nell Wing. It was scribbled in Bill's handwriting; and it appeared to contain material identical to that which Bill had placed in an A.A. Grapevine article. Bill stated there, as "we commenced to form a Society separate from the Oxford Group, we began to state our principles something like this:

> We admitted we were powerless over alcohol.
> We got honest with ourselves.
> We got honest with another person, in confidence.
> We made amends for harms done others.
> We worked with other alcoholics without demand for prestige or money.
> We prayed to God to help us do these things as best we could"

[See Dick B., *The Akron Genesis of Alcoholics Anonymous*, 3rd ed., 1998, pp. 256-57. Identical language—specifying **"we prayed to God"** can be found elsewhere. Not "a" god. Not God as you understand Him. Not whatever kind of God you thought there was. See Bill W., *The Language of the Heart* (NY: The AA Grapevine, Inc. 1988), p. 200; William L. White, *Slaying the Dragon*. (IL: Chestnut Health Systems, 1998), p. 132.]

Time marched on. Bill shifted gears, seemingly bent on putting still more distance between "God," the Akron program about God, and Bill's delegated responsibility to report the original facts in the new text he proposed. And Bill still talked about a "word-of-mouth" program of six steps to achieve and maintain sobriety. But Bill listed a new and rephrased "six steps" as follows; and the dutiful revisionist historians of A.A. followed suit:

> We admitted that we were licked, that we were powerless over alcohol.
> We made a moral inventory of our defects or sins.
> We confessed or shared our shortcomings with another person in confidence.
> We made restitution to all those we had harmed by our drinking.
> We tried to help other alcoholics, with no thought of reward in money or prestige.
> We prayed to whatever God we thought there was for power to practice these precepts.

[See Dick B., *The Akron Genesis*, p. 256; *Alcoholics Anonymous Comes of Age*, p. 160: *"Pass It On,"* p. 197; Ernest Kurtz, *Not-God*. (Center City, MN: Hazelden, 1991), p. 69. Note the prayer to "**whatever God we thought there was**".]

The newly invented six steps were not left alone, however. Others were tinkering with them. This even though there was absolutely no evidence that the Oxford Group had any steps at all – not two, nor four, nor six, nor twelve. But Bill's wife Lois declared that there were "the Oxford Group precepts"—six in number—as follows:

> Surrender your life to God.
> Take a moral inventory.
> Confess your sins to God and another human being.
> Make restitution.
> Give of yourself to others with no demand for return.
> Pray to God for help to carry out these principles.

[See Dick B., *The Akron Genesis*, p. 257; *Lois Remembers* (NY: Al-Anon Family Group Headquarters, 1987), p. 92. Note the language **"surrender to God"** and **"Pray to God"**.].

And then, after Dr. Bob was dead, came the following unsupported insertion in the Big Book. It alleged that Dr. Bob had used "six steps." In language hardly resembling any ever used by Dr. Bob (who had also said *there were no steps*), the Big Book writer attributed the following words to Bob (words containing no mention of God):

Complete deflation.
Dependence and guidance from a Higher Power.
Moral inventory.
Confession.
Restitution.
Continued to work with alcoholics.

(See Dick B., *The Akron Genesis*, p. 258; *Alcoholics Anonymous*, 2d ed., p. 292; *Alcoholics Anonymous Comes of Age*, pp. 22-23; *DR. BOB and the Good Oldtimers*, p. 131).

The Further Burial of Akron Program Ideas in the Words of Bill's New Twelve Steps

This is not a Twelve Step or a Big Book study. My title *Twelve Steps for You* covers the diverse origins of each of the Twelve Steps, examining each, step by step. The Big Book has been extensively studied and well reviewed by such venerable AAs as Joe McQ and Charlie P. in their Seminars, tapes, and books. What's been missing is an understanding of the fact that Bill Wilson was commissioned to write a basic text conveying the program details that were so successful in Akron by 1938. Instead, Wilson and his partner Hank Parkhurst, formed a corporation, drew up a stock prospectus, outlined a completely new and different recovery procedure, and sold the ultimate product as "the steps we took." This despite the fact that there were no steps, that the predecessor Oxford Group had no steps, and that no steps were ever taken by anyone in early 1939—the date the Big Book was published.

As a starting point, we can look at Bill's six word-of-mouth steps and the variant presentations of them. But it is important to highlight the things in the ultimate draft of Twelve Steps that completely changed A.A.'s ideas on what it took to recover. The draft threw Dr. Jung's "conversion" into a barrel and reworded it a "spiritual experience." Here are the highlights (See *Pass It On*, pp, 198-199):

- The idea that AAs were somehow "powerless" replaced the original concept that they were simply "licked." Powerless led more neatly to Bill's "Power." Being licked had been a prelude to a cry to God for help out of the mire.

- The idea that AAs "came to believe" replaced the original concept that they either believed or they didn't. And "Power greater than themselves" replaced the word "God" to appease two or three atheists and fit the step into Bill's "Power" progression.
- The Third Step redefined "sin," characterized it as "self-centeredness," and put a spin on the surrender as being a surrender of self instead of a surrender to God—the kind of surrender involved in a real conversion.
- The Fourth through Seventh Steps involved action to eliminate offensive manifestations of self, rather than adopting the Biblical solution of receiving the spirit of God, walking by the Spirit, and disdaining walk by the flesh. Note the significance of this change in terms of the "cure" concept. "Self" can't be eliminated; hence never "cured." Walking in obedience to God's will is always possible and an attainable condition to cure.
- The restitution aspects of the Eighth and Ninth steps retained the Biblical ideas of agreeing with our adversary quickly, righting wrongs through restoration or reconciliation, and cleansing hands as suggested in James 4:7-10.
- The Tenth and Eleventh Steps shifted attention from a daily walk with the Creator to a daily effort to eliminate self-centeredness plus newly minted defects of character—resentment, self-seeking, dishonesty, and fear. They ignored the Four Absolute standards of Jesus that were so important to AAs and used in Akron—unselfishness, purity, honesty, love.
- The Twelfth Step twisted the needed "conversion" solution to "spiritual experience," but this "solution" no way to a new man in Christ, a new power of the Holy Spirit, and a new relationship with God. Quite frankly, no more dramatic shift in emphasis from God to self can be found elsewhere in the action steps. The Twelfth Step emphasized an experience allegedly produced by action instead of a new creature, in Christ, produced by the Creator in the miracle a new birth. Its message therefore shifted to some undefined experience resulting from the steps taken, rather than a demonstration of what God does for man that man cannot do for himself. It spoke of principles but simply left them unspecified even though, in early A.A., the principles were taken from the Ten Commandments, the

Sermon on the Mount, the Book of James, and 1 Corinthians 13, and other parts of the Bible.

As Bill's Depressions Progressed, Diversionary Programs Multiplied

Clarence Snyder and Cleveland A.A. Perhaps it all started constructively in May, 1939 when Clarence Snyder took the Bible, the Oxford Group Four Absolutes, the Big Book, and the Twelve Steps to Cleveland and made hay with the old and the new, retaining strong ties to both. Cleveland's groups grew from one to thirty in a year. The success rate soared to 93%. And Clarence developed guides to taking the steps and sponsorship. See Three Clarence Snyder Sponsee Old-timers and Their Wives: *Our A.A. Legacy to the Faith Community: A Twelve-Step Guide for Those Who Want to Believe*. Comp. ed. by Dick B. Winter Park, FL: Came to Believe Publications, 2005.

Dr, Bob, Sister Ignatia, and St. Thomas Hospital: In 1940, Akron began to be focused on hospitalization and Twelfth-stepping as part of the work by Dr. Bob and Sister Ignatia at St. Thomas Hospital in Akron. This work retained the important hospitalization of old. But Sister Ignatia added some new approaches, and both Dr. Bob and Anne Smith were moving toward their declining years in energy and effort. The Ignatia story is well covered in Mary C. Darrah. *Sister Ignatia: Angel of Alcoholics Anonymous.* Chicago: Loyola University Press, 1992; and, while it cannot be said that the A.A. program thereby changed, it does seem that a stint with Bob, Ignatia, and St. Thomas might have inclined St. Thomas patients to believe they had completed their rehabilitation even though Akron Group Number One was still meeting, and Dr. Bob was still active.

Enter four new influences. Their respective works are covered elsewhere, but each brought substantial changes to A.A. itself:

(1) Father Ed Dowling, S.J., entered the scene in late 1940; he communicated with Bill for the next twenty years. Their subject matter: Bill's "second conversion" when he did a "fifth step" with Dowling, Dowling's view of the significance of the Exercises of St. Ignatius, and a steady flow of letters. See Robert Fitzgerald. *The Soul of Sponsorship: The Friendship of Fr. Ed Dowling, S.J., and Bill Wilson in Letters*. Hazelden, 1995. But, by 1942, Bill had gone into a deep, severe, almost immobilizing thirteen year depression. And still other leaders and programs were, for whatever reason, attempting to fill the gap.

(2) Richmond Walker had a spotty past as a recycled drunk. He gained an interest in the Oxford Group and its literature as early as 1934. He joined the Oxford Group in 1939 to get sober, but didn't succeed for much over two years. But he gained extensive knowledge of Oxford Group ideas In May of 1942, he entered A.A. and was involved in three very influential literary works. He worked with a devotional titled *God Calling*, which had been edited by Oxford Group writer A.A. Russell. In 1945, a Massachusetts A.A group published Walker's *For Drunks Only* which was filled with Oxford Group ideas, A.A. principles, and sobriety suggestions. He offered it to A.A. for publication and was declined. In 1948, Walker worked with *God Calling* and converted it to a recovery devotional that has sold in the millions, though also declined by A.A. itself. That devotional is titled *Twenty-Four Hours Book*

(3) Father Ralph Pfau Ralph was the first Roman Catholic priest to get sober in Alcoholics Anonymous (he came in on November 10, 1943), and under the pen name which he chose to use, Father John Doe, he wrote his fourteen Golden Books back in the 1940's and 50's and early 60's. They are still being read and used by A.A.'s today: *Spiritual Side* (1947), *Tolerance* (1948), *Attitudes* (1949), and others. They were coming out once a year at the beginning. Then Pfau changed his writing and published three much longer books, including *Sobriety and Beyond* (1955).

(4) Ed Webster: In 1946, in Minneapolis, Ed Webster published *The Little Red Book* under the sponsorship of the A.A. Nicollet Group. Its title was "An Interpretation of the Twelve Steps." Ed had the help and support of Dr. Bob, who gave numerous suggestions for wording various passages. Ed also wrote *Stools and Bottles* (1955), *Barroom Reveries* (1958) and *Our Devilish Alcoholic Personalities* (in 1970, just a year before his death).

Bill's *Twelve Steps and Twelve Traditions*: When Bill finally pulled out of his depression, Anne Smith was dead, Dr. Bob was dead, the reigns of A.A. were becoming the property of New York, and Bill had set about writing a whole new program in his book *Twelve Steps and*

Twelve Traditions. It was heavily edited by two Roman Catholic Jesuit priests who purportedly sought to eliminate Oxford Group thoughts from its content. Bill also introduced a second edition of the basic text and adopted "spiritual awakening" as the target of the steps—leaving conversion, religious experience, and spiritual experience in the dust bin. He completely replaced "conversion" with a psychological conclusion that, for most AAs, a mere personality change sufficient to overcome the "disease" of alcoholism was all that was required for recovery.

Finally, recovery centers and literature substantially pre-empted doctrinal literature publication and distribution. But, as all the foregoing developments occurred, the A.A. success rates became observably more and more dismal—dropping from its original rate of at least 75% to about 5%. And these changes—one and all—provide solid reasons for returning to, re-examining, and learning early ideas and history.

AA OF AKRON rides again through its four later pamphlets commissioned by Dr. Bob

I don't think anything surprised me more as an AA from the West Coast than finding the four AA OF AKRON pamphlets on sale at the Akron A.A. Intergroup Office--pamphlets originally commissioned by Dr. Bob. They had apparently been around for years. They were filled with the kind of Akron A.A. I've described above. They quoted the Bible, recommended prayer, discussed the importance of God, and did so in the context of the Twelve Steps. Yet how in the world did these gems come into being when their contents were virtually unknown where I came from? They seemed at first to be the product or property of some "clandestine A.A." until I learned what I know today—that they closely resembled the Frank Amos summary of early A.A.

I can't say and do not know how much research has been done on their origins. But this much has been suggested. Dr. Bob felt that the program in the Big Book was not easy for "blue collar" AAs to deal with. He asked Evan W. to prepare some practical guides. And four emerged. For those who have become acquainted with early A.A. in Akron, there's not a surprise in them even though two of the four I own were republished, respectively in 1989 and 1993, while the other two were republished in October, 1997.

Treat yourself to this A.A. program material. Program principles and practices that were *not written by Bill W.,* that square with the A.A. that Frank Amos summarized, that frequently quote the Bible—just as Dr. Bob did, and that I described in detail above. And let's look at the general ideas in each of the pamphlets, one by one:

Spiritual Milestones in Alcoholics Anonymous

At the outset, this pamphlet asks and answers the following:

> But, asks the alcoholic, where can I find a simple, step-by-step religious guide? The Ten Commandments give us a set of Thou Shalts and Thou Shalt Nots; the Twelve Steps of AA give us a program of dynamic action; but what about a spiritual guide? Of course the answer is that by following the Ten Commandments and Twelve Steps to the letter we automatically lead a spiritual life, whether or not we recognize it.

Then the pamphlet says: "Here, however, is a set of suggestions, couched in the simplest of language:

> 1 – Eliminate sin from our lives.
> 2 – Develop humility
> 3 – Constantly pray to God for guidance.
> 4 – Practice charity.
> 5 – Meditate frequently on our newly found blessings, giving honest thanks for them.
> 6 – Take God into our confidence in all our acts.
> 7 – Seek the companionship of others who are seeking a spiritual life.

And the explanatory discussions of these seven points frequently mention God, Christianity, the Bible, and prayer. The pamphlet gives several illustrations of how men have found God. It concludes with the Prayer of St. Francis of Assisi.

A Manual for Alcoholics Anonymous

This guide picks up the trail where *Spiritual Milestones* left off. It addresses the newcomer, hospitalization, sponsors, visiting the hospital, and what the newcomer must do on his discharge. He is told to read the Bible and give particular attention to the Sermon on the Mount, Book of James, 1 Corinthians 13, and the Twenty-third and Ninety-first Psalms. The guide suggests a prayer life for each and every day. Then it describes the thrill of helping someone else. Citing Matthew 6:34 of the Sermon on the Mount, it suggests day by day time progress and acquiring health "one day at a time." It quotes Step Twelve as a "Spiritual Experience," not the "Awakening" Bill was soon to substitute as the result of taking the steps.

Second Reader for Alcoholics Anonymous

Its primary topic is, WHAT IS THERE IN AA FOR ME BESIDES SOBRIETY. And the article discusses four items: "Work, Play, Love, and Religion"—substituting A.A. for the latter. It contends that the good active AA is practicing Christianity whether he knows it or not. It devotes a paragraph to the Bible accounts that children loved for years: The Lord's Prayer, David and Goliath and Samson, Adam and Eve in the Garden, the Prodigal Son, and the Good Samaritan. And it lays out some very practical and purposeful ways of sharing a story in A.A. meetings.

A Guide to the Twelve Steps of Alcoholics Anonymous

With this fourth pamphlet, Akron AA completes the circuit of A.A. activity. It offers the following as a simplified, condensed form of the complete program:

- We honestly admitted we were powerless over alcohol and sincerely wanted to do something about it. In other words, we admitted we were whipped and had a genuine desire to QUIT FOR GOOD.
- We asked and received help from a power greater than ourselves and another human. (NOTE: In almost all cases that power is called God. It is, however, God as WE UNDERSTAND HIM. . . .)
- We cleaned up our lives, paid our debts, righted wrongs.

- We carried our new way of life to others desperately in need of it.

The pamphlet discusses each of the Twelve Steps individually. It concludes with these rules for living.

- Remember that you an alcoholic, and but one drink away from drunkenness again.
- Remember that you are completely dependent on God as you understand Him.
- Remember to keep your thinking straight.
- Remember that a wrong act will play on your mind until you either do something to rectify it or get drunk.
- Remember that defects will creep into your life if given half a chance.
- Remember that if only through gratitude, we must help others in order to help ourselves.

Is It Any Wonder!

Just look at the road traveled in A.A. between 1935 and 1955. Just look at how the early Akron A.A. precepts perished a little more along each step of the road. And then ask if it's any wonder that today's people don't even know their history, and perhaps don't even want to know it.

But our educational target is the child of God in A.A.—the Christian, the believer, if you wish—who is awash in authoritative talk about spirituality, higher powers, powerlessness, personality changes, and experiences. It is he who needs to be reached with the simplicity of the early Christian Fellowship program. He has as much at stake in that program as any other person in A.A. It concerns his life, his freedom, and his happiness which were spiraling down the tube in his drinking years. And he has as much need and right as any person in A.A. to know that his own beliefs—when used to deliver him from the power of darkness—were the very beliefs that delivered early AAs from the curse of alcoholism. It was alcohol that was the enemy and the key. And the early pioneers found out how to defeat that enemy and turn the lock with the help of Almighty God.

Part 2

Teach the Puzzled Seeker Some Special Fragments of Early A.A. History and Roots

A View of Bill Wilson as God's on-and-off A.A. Point Man

Who was this Bill Wilson from the tiny village of East Dorset, Vermont? At the very least, we can say that he was a man who devoted himself to the idea that drunks could, like himself, be cured of their terrible curse. The means of cure were the puzzle Bill was called on to discover.

At times, the Creator seemed to send a strong message pointing Bill to the solution. Many many times, Bill had heard the story that his Grandpa Willie Wilson had been a bad drunk. Willie had attended Temperance meetings. He had called out for help at the top of East Dorset's Mount Aeolus. He experienced a dramatic conversion. He rushed to the village Congregational church, seized the pulpit, and told the congregation he had been saved. And Grandpa Willie never had a drink for the rest of his life.

Bill's other Grandpa, Fayette Griffith, provided a different message. Fayette was a quiet man of faith, attended the Congregational Church next door to his home, read his Bible, and supported that church. He figured in the enrollment and attendance by his grandson Bill at the church's Congregational Sunday School. And he fueled Bill's avid interest in reading, including the reading of the Bible.

Young Bill and the Spiritual Wrestling Match

There are many other examples of the prodding the Creator seemed to be giving Bill, and we'll mention some. But there are, perhaps, equally numerous accounts of how a tortured and misguided Bill was often propelled far far away from his Creator's domain—and certainly not by his Creator. Bill was plagued throughout the years with countless severe episodes of depression —one lasting many years from 1942 to 1955. Bill became despondent when his parents separated in his youth. He was in despair when his young sweetheart died unexpectedly. Then the ship of wanderings set him on a different course.

Soon Bill's new bride Lois Burnham exposed him to the spiritualism world in which she and her Swedenborgian family were so steeped; and Bill stayed hooked for decades on that deceptive panacea. Then came his frequent excursions into flagrant adultery. Relieving at best, and yet disgracefully dishonest. Next, Bill was tempted by substantial LSD experiments and didn't quit until his wife, his Secretary, and others had given the drug plenty of whirls. He became obsessed with the idea that niacin was a miraculous vitamin that could eliminate alcoholism. Profit-making shenanigans in A.A. itself steered him off an altruistic course. In fact he was so tempted with love of money that he set up a separate business with his lover Helen and later tried to leave her a chunk of his A.A. royalties—two diversions that required heading off and were in fact eliminated by A.A. leadership. Bill was fatally tempted by tobacco—literally smoking himself to death. And at the end of his life, he once again turned to the temptation of liquor itself.

Midway through his whole life-adventure, Bill made the following perceptive observation: "If there was a devil, he seemed the Boss Universal, and he certainly had me" (*Alcoholics Anonymous*, 4th ed., p. 11).

Whether or not you believe in the devil or in what Jesus had to say in John 10:10 about Jesus's own role, there were repeated examples in Bill's life of what seemed like thunderous knocking at his door by the Almighty amidst determined, side thrust, destructive offers from the Adversary.

Yet Bill's Creator never retired to the bench—all through the wrestling years (See Ephesians 6). Bill had grasped for religious conversion when told of the views of Dr. Carl Jung. Bill reinforced and established his faith in such conversions by his study of William James' book on the subject. He felt sure he had seen, from the life and remarks of his old alcoholic friend Ebby Thacher, that God had done for Ebby what Ebby could not do for himself. He heard for himself that Ebby had truly "got religion"—as Ebby and his companions called it. Then, as Ebby had done, Bill himself went seeking. He headed to Sam Shoemaker's Calvary Rescue Mission, as Ebby had suggested he do. There Bill listened to the Bible, hymns, prayer, and testimonies. Then he answered the altar call, kneeling in prayer at the altar and giving his life to Jesus Christ. This prompted him to write that he too had "got religion" and—in his own words—had "for sure, been born again." Bill received further apparent leading which brought Bill from the Mission to Towns Hospital—there to be hospitalized for the last time. The significance of this last visit to Towns is underlined because it was there where Bill had been indoctrinated by his physician William Duncan Silkworth, M.D., in Silkworth's strongly held belief that Jesus Christ, the Great Physician, could cure drunks. Prior to the Towns visit, Bill had remembered the "Great Physician." At Towns, Bill decided to call on him. And Bill again surrendered and had a conversion experience which he described in words almost identical to those used by Grandpa Willie on Mount Aeolus. Dr. Silkworth and Bill both agreed that Bill had been converted. Bill several times said he never again doubted the power of God. Quite a statement for a man who had once called himself a "conservative atheist."

There were other pulls and tugs in Bill's life. Bill had many long conversations with Reverend Sam Shoemaker of Calvary Church. There was substantial companionship with several of the clergy at Calvary—John Potter Cuyler, W. Irving Harris, Howard Blake, Garrett Stearly, Ray Purdy, and Cleve Hicks. These were soon followed by long conversations with Father Ed Dowling, S.J. Bill had also struck up friendships with Dr. Norman Vincent Peale and Rev. Harry Emerson Fosdick. And, then, in order to complete his titles *Twelve Steps and Twelve Traditions* and *Alcoholics Anonymous Comes of Age*—in a period when Bill was suffering from depression--Bill entered into a working, editorial relationship with Father John C. Ford, S.J. as well as Father Dowling, S.J., to help Bill complete the new A.A. literature. Bill took religious instruction from the famous

Monsignor Bishop Fulton J. Sheen. And all these clergymen seemed to present a phalanx pulling for Bill's believing. Yet all the while Bill was still fellowshipping with his Adversary who repeatedly tempted his honesty in marital and other affairs; weakened his spiritual resolve, suggested idolatrous gods, and in effect dethroned Bill of his position as God's point man. God's messenger, who had so boldly proclaimed to his fellowship his thankfulness that "the Lord has cured me of this terrible disease" (*Alcoholics Anonymous*, 4th ed., p. 191).

The Early Potential for a Recovery Plan Built upon a Rock

There's been a real challenge for those who love A.A., learned its basic text for recovery, and found themselves "recovered" in modern-day A.A. After several years of "sobriety," they begin to examine the tools of recovery. From what have they recovered? Are they now relying on self-sufficiency? Is life without a drink all that appealing when you are buffeted with problems, fears, and failures? Or is there a way to bring the Creator back into the ball game? To learn Who He is. To learn what He put in His owner's manual—the Bible. To learn the full nature and extent of His love, forgiveness, grace, healings, and rules for living according to His will. If you don't think things go better when God draws the building and site plans, then stop reading here. Better, however, consider first that Bill and Bob both said Jesus's Sermon on the Mount contained the underlying philosophy of A.A. And note the following teaching from the Sermon:

> Therefore whosoever heareth these sayings of mine, and doeth them, I will liken him unto a wise man, which built his house upon a rock. And the rain descended, and the floods came, and the winds blew, and beat upon that house; and it fell not: for it was founded upon a rock. And every one that heareth these sayings of mine, and doeth them not, shall be likened unto a foolish man, which built his house upon the sand: And the rain descended, and the floods came, and the winds blew, and beat upon that house; and it fell: and great was the fall of it (Matthew 7:24-27).

Take a look at the rock upon which Bill and Bob together built the original A.A. program. They had no textbook. They had no steps. They believed that the Good Book had the answer to all their problems. In fact, they considered the Sermon on the Mount, the Book of James, and 1 Corinthians 13 to be absolutely essential to their spiritual recovery program.

And if you don't want or like what Bill and Bob did together, you have the choice so many have today. They look back at co-founder Bill and the product he put together in 1939, four years after A.A.'s founding. Bill had no basic text; nor were there any steps. There was not even a consensus as to what Bill's new program should be—religious or psychological? Christian or "universal?" True to Akron's blueprint and the Bible or stripped of Biblical roots? And, whatever your conclusion, ask yourself exactly what Bill did put together? Where did his stuff come from? Who were the contributors? Why were the totality of sources not mentioned by Bill? Was his program "of God"? Why are today's products of Bill's program producing dismal results?

The Shifting Sands of Universalism and Inclusiveness

Bill dodged responsibility for suppressing Akron precepts by asserting that his New York gang was angry, at odds, and irreligious. Though Bill himself had gone to Akron, presented his plan, and obtained a tight but favorable authorization. Though authorized as author, he assumed a new role. Bill said he was just an umpire! Umpire of what? Was he playing for God or for atheists? Was he presenting the Akron program that had succeeded, or trying to placate stockholders of Works Publishing Company—as to which Akron had no connection? Was he trying to pile a hodge podge of old and new ideas into one manuscript in an attempt to please everybody and sell his books?

I don't know of any firm answers to the foregoing questions. I do suggest that, with those questions before you today, you may really only see a foundation on shifting sand—A first step which talks of a quizzical powerlessness instead of being licked. A second step which removed God from its language. A third step which added surrender to "a" god of just about anyone's imagination. A middle group of steps which came from the principle of eliminating sins, but removed the word "sin." Restitution steps which came from the Oxford Group which Bill said had taught AAs more about what not to do than what to do. A daily surrender step which attempted to pull together, without Biblical guides, a daily checking process. A prayer step which came from Quiet Time but rejected all the tools of Quiet Time—new birth, prayer, Bible study, revelation, devotionals, and Christian literature. And a final step (Twelve) so confusing to those who read it that it seemed to shift the "solution"—the finding of God—from Jung's "conversion" to James's "religious experience" to Frank Buchman's "spiritual experience" to Sam Shoemaker's "spiritual awakening" and finally just to a "personality change." With those changes variables, what was there left to believe in at the end of eleven steps? Something? Somebody? Anything, or nothing at all?

I believe this meandering historical confusion makes a strong case for examining the house planned for location upon solid rock. Those who want the entire A.A. picture—to learn the unexpected, and sometimes valueless, shifts in thinking that have occurred, and to be assured of the possibility of cure that the pioneers had—need to look at it all: The sand, the rock, the whole blueprint with changes and extras, the entire construction process, and what happened to the Creator as master-builder.

You may, if you wish, join the ranks of countless people in the religious realm who chide and criticize A.A. for its ineffectiveness, for its absurd names for a god, for the interest of its founders in spiritualism, and for other ungodly conduct primarily involving Bill. But there are, perhaps, as many religious people and clergy who have embraced the good they are convinced has been done by A.A. and by Bill. The real danger is that you may join the ever-increasing hordes of uninformed people in or connected with A.A. who are bending every effort to distance A.A. from religion, marriage, family, church, God, Jesus Christ, Bible, as well as religious dogma and doctrines. Mostly in the name of tolerance, non sectarianism, inclusiveness, universalism, freedom of religion, and even recovery. The A.A. revisionists have, in fact, virtually re-written every aspect of the A.A. program seemingly to make certain that new people never think that, to succeed, they have to believe in God, or even believe in anything at all. Today's new person may likely be met smack dab at the beginning, not with some old codger who tells him that to drink is to die, go insane, or go to jail. Or that God offers the solution.

No. More likely he will hear about a sexual "relationship" someone is suffering through or departing from. His attention will also be quickly arrested by talk of some fantasized "committee" that supposedly meets in the alcoholic's head. Or; he may simply be pondering the strange dilemma of choosing some "higher power" which he has been told can be a door knob, a radiator, a group, or a tree. Even worse, he is often accorded the honor—at twenty days or less of sobriety—of telling a group "how it works." That's assuming he can remember what room he's in, who brought him there, and what the name of the fellowship is. In a word, he has not yet attained academic status—even in A.A. He may not yet have regained his mind.

I'm suggesting in this presentation that you take a long hard look at truth—the truth that offers reliable answers to your needs, weighs your needs against A.A.'s experience, and then enables you to decide for yourself just how much a far more accurate, comprehensive, and truthful history of early A.A. can probably be of real help to you.

What God Made Available to Our Founders

God quickly made it clear, through Ebby, to Bill, the conservative atheist, and to the many who followed Bill that no human power could relieve the alcoholic of his alcoholism and that God could and would, if he were sought. Despite this simple beginning, a new AA member today is confronted at every turn with statements that A.A. is not a religion—though the courts have ruled otherwise; that A.A. is "spiritual, but not religious"—though no one can define the difference; that the A.A. "diety" can be a chair, a light bulb, a table, a radiator, an A.A. group, Good Orderly Direction, Gertrude, or the Big Dipper—though such nonsensical idolatry taxes the understanding of any intelligent listener observer. Wake up. Put on clean glasses. Decide for yourself if you believe anyone ever came to the rooms of Alcoholics Anonymous to find a radiator? Would you, the reader, walk in to an A.A. room suffering from the shakes and bewilderment, hear the word "tree," and rush to the door to pray to the nearest tree for relief of your alcoholism?

Instead, let's hope you catch a glimpse of the Twelve Steps hanging on the wall. Hope you'll see the word "God." Hope you'll see the word "unmanageable"—as it seems to refer to you and others. Hope you'll hear someone say, "Let go, and let God." Hope you'll see a step that talks about God's will and God's power. If that is your experience, I believe you will conclude in a matter of seconds that you are in a room which offers some kind of solution to excessive drinking, and suggests that God has some answers for you. Let's start there—with you!

How a New A.A. Way Can Work in Company with God

What's the suggestion today? You don't need to organize, staff, and lead a crusade and invade A.A. with evangelism. Nor would you want to demand a vote that will return A.A. to its early Christian Fellowship. God forbid. A.A. knowingly abandoned its Christian status within a few years of its founding. There is no point at all today in trying to reverse that and change A.A.

But there's another way in to the newcomer's heart and another way out of the confusion and unbelief that confronts him. There is a way out of the dilemma the confused Christian member, new or otherwise, faces as his mind begins to clear, reality beckons, and life offers new choices. The new way in, and the new way out, have to do with the individual AA. Not with his meetings. Not with his sponsor. Not with the speaker. Not with the Big Book. Not with the slogans. Not with the Traditions. Not with his residual treatment center jargon. Not with what he hears some speaker say. And not with his vote. Nobody's looking for his vote or his approval or his opinion. Hopefully, everyone is looking for his recovery as A.A.'s primary purpose.

There is a new way in, and a new way out, for one of God's kids in today's A.A.—the way that requires no effort for you or me evangelize or convert. Rather, the way that will show Christians and others who are awash in godless thinking, what they can do with God's help—just as the pioneers did. Just as there's no call for you or me to convert some new individual, there's no call for religious people or for the religious community to convert an AA or his group to some religious denomination. A.A. never was a denomination, and probably never wanted to be. The New Way Out is a way in—an approach in the fellowship by which the truthful, important, religious ideas that were involved in A.A.'s founding—are brought to the doorstep of every child of God inside A.A. and 12 Step programs today. A way that will encourage everyone within A.A.'s membership to be just as teachable, viable, welcoming, hospitable, and effective today as the pioneers were in the 1930's. Their approach then was showing the pigeon how to fly, not shooting him down for his beliefs.

This proposed new, one-on-one instruction, should insure "freedom of information." That means you really inform an AA, his fellowship, and his church exactly how the three inter-related groups can complement each other. They tried to do that in the 1930's. Why not now! There's a lot of difference between indoctrinating someone with your views and informing someone of the truth. In this case, the truth about early A.A. The key is how to differentiate. And the new way strongly suggests that AAs themselves abide firmly by four of their most strongly expressed principles:

(1) Love and tolerance is our Code.
(2) The steps, simmered to their essence, amount to love and service.
(3) We have stopped fighting anybody or anything.
(4) Our real purpose is to fit ourselves to be of maximum service to God and the people around us.

You'll find the four precepts in the Big Book and A.A. literature. Relying on Biblical principles overcomes fear of another's views.

Again, this is not about a battle to drive Christians into, or out of A.A. Not as seen by most churches, clergy, professionals, treatment programs, treatment centers. Not even by atheists, bigots, nor egotists. The real battle needs victory in silencing all the above in recovery rooms. It's a battle that strives for silence when it comes to comments against an individual AA's beliefs, words, questions, and religious convictions. And to his need and right to be free from intimidation, castigation, ridicule, and words that shame or inflame him.

Now that does not cover the whole battle. The rest of it is to eliminate stupidity, ignorance, anger, and insult. The newcomer has a need and a right to hear about *all* of A.A. To hear about how some drunk stopped drinking. To hear how some nut got released from the mental ward. To hear how some criminal got out of jail. To hear about the alcohol and drugs and excesses that were involved in putting them there. And then to tell his own story, from his own point of view, as to exactly how he did what the Twelve Steps suggested—Found that, by his own power, defeating alcohol was too much for him. Found that A.A. suggested resort to one power—Almighty God. Found that he was strongly urged to find God at once. And then found that the Twelve Steps were suggested—not mandated, not directed, not required, not even necessary—as an AA's program of recovery. Not to parrot the program of a court, a judge, a sponsor, a therapist, a speaker, a clergyman, a physician, or a psychologist. Found that A.A. said it was going to talk about God, claimed no monopoly on God, not even on methods of recovery. Found that A.A. was based on what worked—not what was suggested. Found that early AAs relied on God. Found that early AAs accepted Christ. Found that early AAs tried to eliminate sin from their lives. Found that early AAs studied the Bible, prayed, read religious literature, and asked God's guidance for a life in obedience to God's will. Found that early AAs were cured. And found that the end was just the beginning. The pioneer's cure was his signal to help someone else to a cure—with God's power. That's the newcomer's right. It is not being jealously protected. It's not being faithfully upheld today by many A.A. leaders, speakers, and members. And if that doesn't change, lives will be lost; minds will be destroyed; freedom will vanish; flight to other successful avenues will become frequent; and, if it changes, the bottom line will not be whether insurance pays for this or that program, but which program lays it on the line as to God, history, and the Bible's truths. Truths about healing, forgiveness, love, service, tolerance, and peace. Truth as to which program had the 75% successes. And which program continues to report only a 5% success rate.

Love and tolerance help newcomers. They help all of us. Love and service spell out the approach to newcomers. Without it, most of us would never have made it inside the front door. Fighting—fighting a newcomer's religion, his church, his Bible, his belief in God, his walk in the steps of Jesus Christ—introduces conduct that was thoroughly repugnant in early A.A. Likewise, conduct that rejects the love of God and the love of our neighbor violates these commandments early AAs studied in their Bibles:

> Hear, O Israel; The Lord our God is one Lord: And thou shalt love the Lord thy God with all thy heart, and with all thy soul, and with all thy mind, and with all thy strength: this is the first commandment. And the second is like, namely, this, Thou shalt love thy neighbor as thyself. There is none other commandment greater than these (Mark: 12:29-31).

If some AA thinks it his privilege to quiet a religious remark, or to expel a religious member, or to quote Traditions to a shaking Christian newcomer, he's tampering with a life; and he's sure not my A.A. friend. However high he may have climbed the leadership ladder, he's slipped to the bottom rung. A.A. is about saving lives. A.A. today is about welcoming the unwanted, the sick, the needy, the ignorant, and even the bigot. But many AAs today are throwing rocks at God, at religion, at A.A.'s own history, and, more than often, at someone in their own fellowship. Not surprisingly, in response, many Christians and Christian churches are either criticizing A.A., urging members to flee from it, or organizing mimic groups with Christian labels. Yet church attendance was favored in Akron.

But why join or support either gang. Focus on the guy who is not a gang member, the guy who just walked in the door, the guy who looks like he needs help and friendship in the worst possible manner. There is an appropriate way to meet this guy. It's a way which can and should appeal to those who want to help, who want to love and serve, and who want to implement their own religious knowledge and beliefs. The New Way Out—really the new way in to the confused Christian in A.A.—needs to be pursued by every caring Christian AA and by every caring Christian church as well. Its target is the newcomer who needs a relationship with God so very badly, realizes it, and will work for it. Its tools require emphasis on early A.A.'s reliance on the Bible, and on the Bible's clear instructions as to how to bring a believer into fellowship with his Father. Information jeopardizes no person, no sobriety, and nobody's beliefs.

And this is where religion can shine, if asked. The Gospel was about news, not views. And A.A. is where Christian AAs can touch Christian newcomers who want to be touched. A.A. pioneers were students, not teachers; they were taught, not teaching; and they were changed by God, not by changing others through some self-made religion.

It may be that you don't like this kind of help for the Christian newcomer? Then don't provide it. And perhaps you'll get a coffee pot, find a friend, take your prejudice to some meeting of your own choosing, and never take a drink just like the rest of us.

Teach the Willing What They Have Been Given

Again, the confused Christian newcomer is our target. He's the one to be reached and rescued from a cesspool of criticism and insults This is a call for teaching history. The listeners can then decide on their faith, if they choose. But they will be enabled to choose after hearing truth, not criticism; receiving love, not intolerance; being motivated by the love of God and service to God that glorifies Him, not intimidation; and armed with an ability to cut through crude, ignorant criticisms, and see the primary purpose that was and is to help those who still suffer. And who will thankfully hear and receive a way out that enables them to come to the Father through His son Jesus Christ in accordance with their faith, and still stand tall as AAs who need support, friendship, and an outlet for real service to others with like pains. Christian helpers are just as vital to effective recovery work as any paid "trusted servant."

Part 3

Tell the Newcomer The Pioneers Were Cured. Ask, Why not You?

Most of us, and that certainly includes me, did not come to A.A. to fight, criticize, render opinions, or evangelize. We came, as we should to any professional helper—doctor, dentist, nurse, accountant, plumber, auto mechanic, or policeman. We came to them as professionals, experts, or both. And AAs are seldom professionals—not paid, not trained, not looking for an A.A. job, not running for office, and not spoiling for a good fight. We came, as we need to come, to be helped and cured, and then to help others. Our help came from God. So did our cure. The labor came from volunteers. And the victory was demonstrated when the next in line started getting our attention.

Start with the Power of God, His Cures, and What AAs Themselves Claimed about God's Role When A.A. was Founded

The principle that alcoholism can be cured by the power of God was accepted and applied long before the Society of Alcoholics Anonymous was founded in 1935. Moreover, God's role in His creation involves far more than curing alcoholism. One can look at Psalm 103 and see that His benefits have included healing of all diseases, forgiving all iniquities, redeeming lives from destruction, showering His children with kindness and tender loving mercies. And there was much more to come—an abundant life, receipt of the spirit of God, acquittal from guilt, healing, power, comfort, and all the rest, not to forget salvation from the wrath to come and everlasting life with the Father. So you don't start with what God can't do. You don't limit His role to that of a healing physician. You start with Who He is, why He does what He does. And what He wants for everyone in the world.

If you get entangled with those who don't care about our Heavenly Father and His will, don't get angry. Read Dr. Bob's commentary on page 181 of the Big Book and his feeling sorry for such critics. And then just find someone who does care.

In Appendix Three of my book *When Early AAs Were Cured and Why*, I wrote a piece titled "Miracles Not to Be Forgotten" (pp. 143-59). As thoroughly as space permitted, I laid out the astonishing number of miracles recorded in the Bible. The Bible itself qualifies as the first miracle. The Old Testament is filled with miracles and healings performed by Yahweh the Creator. No less impressive are the signs, miracles, wonders, healings, and resurrections of the dead accomplished by Jesus, his apostles, and his disciples and recorded in the four Gospels. Then the great mystery is revealed: There could be and were healings recorded in the Book of Acts by or for those who choose to become born again of God's spirit and perform the same miracles that Jesus performed and promised they could perform because he was going to his Father. They acted in the name of Jesus Christ and employed the power of the Holy Spirit which the crucifixion, burial, and resurrection of Jesus had enabled them to receive. Though it became popular a while back for some to claim the "Age of Miracles" was gone, the accounts of miracles continue through apostolic times, healings by church fathers, and healings within the church for some 2,000 years thereafter. My documented material also specifies the healings by the power of God that have been accomplished from 1,800 to date, many of which were actually recorded and detailed in books on healing that A.A. co-founder Dr. Bob studied and circulated among early AAs and their families.

God Didn't Somehow Get Disarmed When It Came to Helping Alcoholics

What about alcoholism? Faced with that malady, did the Creator of the heavens and the earth lose His long-recorded ability to perform signs, miracles, and wonders that seemed humanly impossible? Was God somehow uniquely limited in His power and ability to help alcoholics and addicts?

A host of writers about, observers of, and members in, 12 Step groups—seldom acclaimed as clergy or experts in treating alcoholics—seem to have swarmed to these conclusions. All in less than a century and all appearing to hive after one or two rank amateurs who captured the attention of the uninformed and of those who sought to profit from revolving door treatments.

But there were many who rejected that erroneous negativity. They could be found in a variety of arenas. And let's start with the famous Zurich psychiatrist named Carl Jung. As Wilson biographer Susan Cheever wrote:

> During his unsuccessful treatment of Rowland [Hazard], Jung told him that most alcoholics are hopeless cases. He added that the only cures he had seen with alcoholism were through spiritual experiences [Susan Cheever. *My Name is Bill.* (NY: Washington Square Press, 2004), p. 112]

Actually, Jung referred to conversions—not experiences; and this conversion concept won him the title bestowed by Bill Wilson. Jung, said Bill, was a founder of A.A. and the person who provided it with a name for the spiritual solution to alcoholism—conversion.

The next affirmation of belief in God's power came in the voluminous, complex writing by William James, *The Varieties of Religious Experience*. James had waded through all kinds of famous "conversions"—voluntary, gospel, self-surrender, and more—and affirmed their reality whether or not they are attributed to the power of God or to psychological change. For this conclusion and a couple of others less persuasive, Wilson also awarded the long-dead James the title of founder of A.A. And it certainly was Professor James, said Wilson, who provided AAs with scholarly proof of conversions that had occurred, that they included the variety mentioned by Jung, and that Bill Wilson's conversion observations were "real."

Then came two more men, who were related to A.A. itself. They were the doctors William D. Silkworth and Harry Tiebout. Wilson biographer Cheever had this to say about their views:

> Although many medical professionals now recommend Alcoholics Anonymous to patients who have drinking problems, the relationship between A.A. and the medical profession was less than friendly at first. With

> some exceptions—Dr. Silkworth and later Dr. Harry Tiebout—doctors resisted the idea that alcoholism could be cured by some kind of spiritual awakening, or even by meetings with other alcoholics (Cheever, *Bill W.*, p. 162)

The recent biography of Silkworth put it much more explicitly, boldly and directly:

> Silkworth has not been given the appropriate credit for his position on a spiritual conversion, particularly as it may relate to Christian benefits. Several sources, including Norman Vincent Peale in his book *The Positive Power of Jesus Christ*, agree that it was Silkworth who used the term "The Great Physician" to explain the need in recovery for a relationship with Jesus Christ [Dale Mitchel, *Silkwort*h: *The Little Doctor Who Loved Drunks* (Center City, MN: Hazelden, p. 50]

A.A.'s Physicians and Founders Quickly Saw that God's Power Produced The Cures Medicine had Failed to Achieve

Jung, James, Silkworth, and Tiebout all attributed to conversion the cure upon which AAs relied. And that is precisely what each of A.A.'s three founders also made clear. Both Bill Wilson and Bill Dotson, A.A. Number Three, said that the Lord had been so wonderful "curing [them] of this terrible disease that [they] just [wanted] to keep telling people about it". (*Alcoholics Anonymous*, 4th ed., p. 191). Dr. Bob was the first to say that Bill Wilson had "been cured by the very means I had been trying to employ, that is to say the spiritual approach" (*A.A., 4th* p.180). Then, when Bill and Bob were looking for a drunk to help, "Bob phoned Akron City Hospital and explained to the nurse in the receiving ward that a man from New York had just found a cure for alcoholism. . . . that he [Bob] had tried it, and that it involved working with other alcoholics" (*Pass It On*, pp. 152-153). Making quite firm his opinion as to God's being the source of cures, Bob ended his personal story with this assurance: "Your Heavenly Father will never let you down!" (*Alcoholics Anonymous*, 4th ed., p. 181).

But such affirmations didn't end with the founders or the doctors just mentioned. I have in my possession copies of hundreds of newspaper and magazine articles covering the period from 1935 through the next ten years and stating in the words of AAs all over the United States that they had been cured of their malady. And they weren't hesitant to credit God.

The Nix on the Creator as Healer was Promoted by Uninformed Amateurs and Doubters

It was not until a lay therapist named Richard Peabody (who later died drunk) wrote a book titled *The Common Sense of Drinking* that the "no cure" nix seemed to be imposed on the alcoholic. Almost out of the blue, Bill Wilson adopted two basic ideas from Peabody's book. These were destined to change A.A. for the worse and to feed the treatment industry patient rolls for decades to come. The two expressions were "We are not cured of alcoholism" (*A.A.* 4th, p. 85) and "Once an alcoholic always an alcoholic" (A.A. 4th, p. 33). And both statements are dead wrong.

Yet if you write or say to most AAs today that alcoholism can be cured, they are likely to shun you like a leper. They just don't know that, for a decade, almost every single AA and A.A. article was talking about cure. I get phone calls every now and then from some such who insist that I am not cured—despite my robust, cheery, firm statement that I am. And the protest reasons seem to be several:

(1) They either don't know or don't believe what early AAs were regularly reading from the Bible: "And all things, whatsoever ye shall ask in prayer, believing, ye shall receive." Matthew 21:22.
(2) They either don't know or don't believe that God has the power to do the things He says He will do. As to which Jesus taught: "Ye do err, not knowing the scriptures, nor the power of God." Matthew 22:29
(3) They either don't know or don't believe the truth of what the angel said to Mary: "For with God nothing shall be impossible." (Luke 1:37)

It's an either or proposition, just like the one both Sam Shoemaker and Bill Wilson flatly stated in their writings: "God either is, or He isn't."

And God either has the power the Bible says He has, or He doesn't. In fact, it was Bill Wilson himself who said after he was converted in Towns Hospital that he never again doubted the power of God.

If Bill didn't doubt the power of God, then why on earth did he adopt the Peabody nonsense that there is no cure, while at the same time proclaiming that he (Bill Wilson) had been cured? Frankly, I don't know. But I do know this: Most people who have suffered from alcoholism are strangely immune to seeing the consequences their own histories make enticing and inevitable. They may have been cured of an allergy, an obsession, and a progressive spiritual malady. But no one has taken away their choice. They can be tempted and drink too much. They can remember too little and drink too much. They can remember a lot and drink too much. They can be risk takers and drink too much. And most have not lost their memories, or forgotten their habits or completely renounced their weak abilities to resist the devil and to resist temptation. I'll let the theologians take up the issue of why a believer serves sin when Christ has made him free from sin. But one story at the end of the First Edition of the Big Book gets mighty close to the answer. It quotes from Paul in Romans 7:24: "O wretched man that I am! Who shall deliver me from the body of this death? I thank God through Jesus Christ our Lord. So then with the mind I myself serve the law of God; but with the flesh the law of sin." I'd suggest that no matter how much has been accomplished for those who are in Christ Jesus, they can still serve the law of God with their mind or the law of sin with their flesh. And nobody knows better than the devil how to offer that choice. I'm cured of alcoholism, but I choose to stand, to resist, and not to let the devil propose a choice I know is deadly. The key is *choice*!

Remember those two terrible curses belatedly laid upon Christians, newcomers, and all AAs alike. They are told—one and all—: We are not cured of alcoholism and once an alcoholic always an alcoholic. This negative, faithless, fear-oriented doctrine has been so powerful through the years that it has caused unbelieving AAs to change literature, change descriptions, and attempt to change or at least to bury the early history of exactly what Almighty God did for their founders.

You Can't Believe in God and Ignore Early A.A. History

Why should we resurrect and underline the prevalent, remarkable revisionist writing about our supposedly incurable disease? The reasons are several: (1) The statements are false; and they deserve to be spotlighted and then buried. (2) They fly in the face of a decade of declarations by AAs that cures had been accomplished and were available. (3) They seem derived from phony and bizarre ideas that came neither from A.A. sources, nor from medicine, nor from religion, nor even from scientific studies of earlier years: Those phony ideas are these: (a) Bill Wilson fashioned out of thin air the idea you could make the A.A. group your "higher power" if you wished. Yet who would then expect to be cured by a group! (b) This "higher power" idolatry cannot be found in the Bible, but it is the darling of those who have chosen to broaden "God" to mean a radiator, a light bulb, the Big Dipper, Ralph, a Coke bottle, a chair, and a host of other nonsensical figures and figurines. In fact, some on A.A.'s paid staff regularly write that you can believe your higher power is "Something" or "Somebody" or nothing at all. Yet who would want to put his cure in the hands of nothing at all? The absurdity of such thinking is beyond reason (c) The foregoing self-made religion and absurd names for a god have been turned into scholarly, theological dogma by a former alcoholic priest become scholar who wrote a dissertation classifying A.A. as "not-god-ness." This characterization finds no support in A.A. history, but the priest has become the darling of academia and is quoted at every turn by those involved in grant research, technical articles, and scientific studies. This idolatry has seldom been challenged by AAs due to ignorance of their own history and complacency about cure and God's power. Nor has the idolatry often been challenged even by many religious writers including those who either reject A.A. as heretical or idolatrous or simply do not know its early history, Biblical roots, and original Christian fellowship. These commentators simply fluff off A.A. theology as convoluted but practical—with no citation establishing the practicality of a belief that those who rely on light bulbs are almost universally cured of drunkenness! I eagerly await the day we will finally hear an AA or a scholar saying aloud, "That's absurd. It's nuts. It's crazy. And it will get someone drunk if they rely on it." Do statistics show that reliance on a radiator will be no defense against the first drink? I doubt any scholar would even ask.

If, therefore, an individual AA such as myself, or a group of AAs, or a group of 12 Step activists, or a Christian recovery or treatment group, clergy, or inquiring scholars and physicians are to find God in A.A. at all today, they are going to have to clarify that God is not dead; that He is the one, true, living Creator; that He is the power to which A.A. pioneers turned for cure; and that He made available the power that cured them.

The preponderance of evidence about the nature, principles, practices, and value of A.A. lies with its original thesis: A.A. has no monopoly on God, but it is founded on the principle that a cure is attained through conversion and the establishment of a relationship with the "One who has all power"—God as AAs specifically described Him in the preface to their suggested Twelve Steps of Recovery.

In fact, if one delves into recovery history far enough, he or she should become convinced that the Godly principles in the early A.A. Christian Fellowship—even the words "Creator," "Maker," "Father," and "God"—were those which had been taken from the Bible and used for centuries to help alcoholics get well.

Is it any wonder, then, that we suggest that you include in your statements, your leads, and your program a chapter of history so that AAs and patients and sponsors can get their act together, learn their original program, recognize the revisionist substitutes, and then march on with Big Book, Bible, Twelve Steps, and a newcomer in hand, showing the new person how people got cured in "Old School A.A." Then it's up to him. He can make an informed choice. And make up his own god? I don't think so.

Part 4

For Facts about Why Early A.A. Succeeded, Look at the Successful Power Houses That Preceded and Influenced It

Example Number One: The United Christian Endeavor Society. Organized in 1881, about the time of Dr. Bob's birth. Focused on the young people in a local Protestant Church which was supported by the Christian Endeavor Group connected with that church. The young people, including those in the Society to which Dr. Bob belonged at the North Congregational Church in St. Johnsbury, Vermont, were practicing almost all the major ideas that were carried over into early Akron A.A.'s Christian Fellowship led by Dr. Bob. The ideas? Confession of Christ. Bible study. Prayer meetings. Conversion meetings. Quiet Hours, topical discussions, reading of religious literature, witness, and fellowship—all under the banner of "love and service." Christian Endeavor's membership was world-wide and exceeded 3,500,000. See Dick B., *The James Club and The Early A.A. Program's Absolute Essentials; The Good Book-Big Book Guidebook; Making Known the Biblical History and Roots of Early A.A.; A New Way Out.*

Example Number Two: The Salvation Army. Organized under General William Booth not long after Christian Endeavor and plunged into helping homeless, outcasts, drunks, and street criminals. Their unselfish service work proved the success of abstinence, resisting temptation. confessing Jesus Christ as Saviour, relying on the Creator for guidance and strength, eliminating sin. Then effectively employing the power of one saved and recovered outcast to bring home to another still-suffering the message of salvation, love, and service. Also perpetuating fellowship and witness among those already saved, recovered soldiers. Weighing both the strengths and limitations of the Salvation Army with its 10,000 centers, various kinds of ministries carried on by 5,200 officers and 32,000 workers, the Rev. Dr. Howard Clinebell believes that the Army represents evangelistic therapy at its best and that some facilities have remarkable success in getting and keeping countless former homeless, low-bottom addicts sober and living constructive lives. Howard Clinebell. *Understanding and Counseling Persons with Alcohol, Drug, and Behavioral Addictions* (Nashville: Abingdon Press, 1998), pp. 157, 159. See also Dick B., *When Early AAs Were Cured and Why; The First Nationwide A.A. History Conference; A New Way Out.*

Example Number Three: Rescue and Gospel Missions. There are hundreds of missions today, and there were many in early A.A. days—providing "soup, soap, and salvation" to thousands upon thousands of down-trodden homeless and inebriate people. Both Bill Wilson and his sponsor Ebby Thacher went to Calvary Church's Rescue Mission; and both were aware of the evangelistic activities involving Bible teaching, prayer, hymns, and altar calls where Jesus Christ was accepted as Saviour. Though the records have been buried today, it is clear that many of the original New York A.A. manuscript materials contained "dogma and doctrines" from the mission programs. All were used and mentioned in the activities in Akron and even in New York. See Dick B. *A New Way Out, The Conversion of Bill W.*

Example Number Four: The conversion ideas of Dr. Carl Gustav Jung. Two or three historians who have not really done their homework now claim that Jung had no connection with A.A.'s beginnings. They assert that Jung never saw Rowland Hazard as a patient and therefore the "conversion" solution so dominant in Bill Wilson's Big Book program did not come from Jung. But such skimpy research has now been superseded. Moreover, it never did support the absurd conclusion that Jung, Rowland Hazard, Ebby Thacher, Bill Wilson, and Sam Shoemaker all lied in order to conjure up a solution. The real problem concerns how badly Wilson missed the point of Jung's idea of conversion. Conversion, Jung said, was the solution for Rowland's chronic alcoholism. But conversion, to Jung, did not mean what the Bible describes as a new birth and which Shoemaker and the Akronites were later espousing. Nor was Bill Wilson's response to the altar call at Shoemaker's Calvary Mission a conversion of the kind Jung had in mind. Nonetheless "conversion" became the foundational solution Wilson proposed for alcoholism, and Jung was called by Bill a "founder" of A.A. See *New Light on Alcoholism: God, Sam*

Shoemaker, and A.A.; Twelve Steps for You; The Good Book-Big Book Guidebook; The Conversion of Bill W.

Example Number Five: Professor William James and the "spiritual experience." Just who is the author of Bill's "spiritual experience" expression is not all that clear. Carl Jung told Rowland Hazard that Rowland needed a "conversion" experience. William James wrote *Varieties of Religious Experience*, which Wilson believed validated his "hot flash" experience—possibly a "spiritual experience"—at Towns Hospital. Finally, as he looked back on his life, Bill Wilson concluded he had had five spiritual experiences—possibly six if you accept his statement that his confessions to Father Dowling amounted to another "conversion experience." These experiences are covered in my forthcoming title, *The Conversion of Bill W.* Reverend Sam Shoemaker wrote in his first book *Realizing Religion* that people needed a "vital religious experience." Oxford Group writings are surfeited with references to "spiritual experience" and "spiritual awakening." So are Shoemaker's later books. Wilson liked to attribute the spiritual experience idea to James, an experience following "deflation-at-depth." Wilson also dubbed James a "founder" of A.A. And I certainly can and did find the James ideas Wilson mentioned and underlined the material in my titles *Turning Point: A History of Early A.A.'s Spiritual Roots and Successes* and *The Conversion of Bill W.*

Example Number Six: The role of Dr. Silkworth as a "founder" of A.A. has assumed new and far greater importance of late because of recent research into Silkworth's views about the cure of alcoholism by Jesus Christ and conversations he had with Wilson to that effect. There were also the medical ideas of Dr. William D. Silkworth. Once again, historians who have not really done their homework, sometimes claim that Dr. Silkworth did not originate the concept of alcoholism as a disease. To be sure, the disease concept itself has been challenged, and it may well not have originated with Silkworth. But there is equally strong evidence that it was Silkworth who spelled out for Bill Wilson the idea that Wilson was suffering from a mental obsession and a physical allergy—however the details were or would be characterized in a disease debate. Virtually unmentioned by historians, however, is Silkworth's belief—explained to Bill Wilson and other patients—that Jesus Christ, the "Great Physician," could cure them of alcoholism. Dick B. *The Good Book-*

Big Book Guidebook, The Conversion of Bill W.; Peale, *The Positive Power of Jesus Christ;* Mitchel. *Silkworth—The Little Doctor Who Loved Drunks.*

Example Number Seven: The Oxford Group—A First Century Christian Fellowship. Not really "organized" until about 1919 when the book *Soul Surgery* was first published. Primarily a movement which drew its life-changing ideas from Biblical concepts of Lutheran Minister Frank N. D. Buchman. Each one of the aforementioned examples influenced various ideas that were borrowed and adapted by the Akron program. And to these were added catch-words and ideas that Buchman picked up during his group's actual founding. There were **twenty-eight ideas** in all that impacted upon A.A.'s Big Book and Twelve Steps and existed in greater or lesser degree in some of the practices in the earlier Akron Fellowship. The 28 ideas can be summarized in **eight groupings**: (1) **God**—descriptions of Him, His plan, man's duty, believing. (2) **Sin**—that which blocks us from God and others. (3) **Surrender**—the decision to surrender self and self-will to God's will. (4) **Life-changing art**—the Five C's process moving from Confidence to Confession to Conviction to Conversion to Continuance. (5) **Jesus Christ**—His power and the Four Absolute Standards. Buchman said: Sin was the problem. Jesus Christ was the cure. And the result was a miracle. (6) **Growth in fellowship** through Quiet Time, Bible study, prayer, and seeking Guidance. (7) **Restitution—for the harms caused by sin.** (8) **Fellowship and witness**—working in teams loyal to Jesus Christ to change the lives of others. Though Wilson was inclined for years to minimize and side-step the Oxford Group influence on the Big Book and Twelve Steps, the facts show otherwise. The Oxford Group ideas constitute the entire action part of Bill's step program. See Dick B. *The Oxford Group and Alcoholics Anonymous: A Design for Living That Works; The Akron Genesis of Alcoholics Anonymous; Turning Point: A History of the Spiritual Roots and Successes of Alcoholics Anonymous; A New Way Out; Twelve Steps for You.*

Example Number Eight: The teachings of Episcopalian priest Rev. Samuel M. Shoemaker, Jr. Sam teamed up with Frank Buchman about 1919 and then began writing an incredibly large series of books on OG ideas and Sam's Bible concepts. Sam headquartered his efforts at Calvary Church in New York, of which he became Rector in 1925. It is fair to say that the most quoted, the most copied, and the most persuasive influence on Bill Wilson and his Big Book approach came directly from Shoemaker. So said Bill himself. To the point where Wilson actually asked Sam to write the Twelve Steps, as to which Sam declined in favor of their being written by an alcoholic, namely, Bill. See Dick B. *New Light on Alcoholism: God, Sam Shoemaker, and A.A.; The First Nationwide History Conference; When Early AAs Were Cured and Why; By the Power of God; Twelve Steps for You.*

Example Number Nine: The lay therapy ideas of Richard Peabody. Dr. Bob and Bill Wilson both owned and studied *The Common Sense of Drinking*—a book by lay therapist Richard Peabody. And though Peabody died drunk, Wilson somehow saw fit to adopt almost verbatim certain words and phrases from the Peabody book. Among the two most unfortunate derivatives were: (1) There is no cure for alcoholism. (2) Once an alcoholic always an alcoholic. Both concepts flew in the face of a decade of clear and outspoken declarations by the early AAs and their observers that they had found a cure for alcoholism that rested on the power of Jesus Christ. Peabody simply didn't embrace Christianity as part of his therapy. And how Wilson got switched from God to incurable illness on the basis of the writings of a lay therapist who died drunk is currently a mystery to me. See Richard Peabody. *The Common Sense of Drinking;* Dick B. *Cured: Proven Help for Alcoholics and Addicts; When Early AAs Were Cured and Why; A New Way Out.*

Example Number Ten: The Biblical Emphasis from Dr. Bob's youth and Christian Endeavor contrasted with the New York influence from Sam Shoemaker. A.A. detractors and doctrinaire Christians who dislike the Oxford Group seem impelled to claim that A.A. came from the Oxford Group, that the Oxford Group was an heretical cult, and that its very existence was an example of what A.A. wasn't, rather than what it was. And these canards are so heavily entrenched in A.A. religious and recovery thinking and writing they may never be dispelled. But they are fallacious and utterly misleading. If you are a student of Oxford Group writings, you simply can't escape the obvious: Bill Wilson's Big Book and Twelve Step program embraced almost every Oxford Group idea—even though Bill Wilson used several ruses which were meant to deny the fact. By contrast, the early Akron program, which produced the 75 to 93% success rates, really had very little to do with Oxford Group missions, principles, and practices. The Akron focus was on abstinence—not an Oxford Group idea; hospitalization—not an Oxford Group idea; resisting temptation—not an Oxford Group idea; accepting Jesus Christ as Lord and Saviour—not an Oxford Group requirement; relying on the Creator for strength and guidance—a universal idea undoubtedly embraced by the Oxford Group; Bible study meetings—not an Oxford Group emphasis; old-fashioned prayer meetings—not an Oxford Group idea; Quiet Time—a universal idea which pre-dated the Oxford Group and was a big item in Christian Endeavor, the YMCA, and the Oxford Group; religious comradeship—not an Oxford Group idea; favored church attendance—not an Oxford Group idea; love and service as a banner—not an Oxford Group expression, and clearly Christian Endeavor words of art; working with others—not an Oxford Group emphasis when it came to alcoholism, nor was it particularly a Christian Endeavor idea except as to witnessing and conversion. By contrast, the simple Christian Endeavor program appears to represent the heart of what Akron did and what it was reported in official A.A. literature to have done. That program was not incorporated in the Big Book, but it is reported fully in Frank Amos' reports to John D. Rockefeller, Jr., that are part of A.A.'s Conference-approved literature. See my titles Dick B. *The First Nationwide A.A. History Conference; The Good Book and The Big Book: A.A.'s Roots in the Bible; Why Early A.A. Succeeded (A Bible study primer); The Good Book-Big Book Guidebook*; *The James Club and The Early A.A. Program's Absolute Essentials; A New Way Out; Twelve Steps for You.*.

Example Number Eleven: The practical records and teachings of Dr. Bob's Wife. How A.A. could have buried Anne Smith's role, her importance, and her spiritual journal is a complete mystery. The facts about Anne's importance would stand on their own even if she had never written her journal which spanned nine of A.A.'s formative years. As far as I've been able to discover, Bill never ever mentioned Anne's journal. Yet Bill Wilson and many pioneers called Anne the "Mother of A.A." The pioneer AAs were housed in her home from the beginning, and those AAs got well. AAs were fed in her home, and it became the first real "half-way" house after hospitalization. Anne read the Bible to A.A.'s founders and to the many who followed them. Anne conducted a quiet time each morning at the Dr. Bob's Home where she led a group of AAs and their families in Bible study, prayer, listening, and topical discussions. Anne counseled and nursed and taught alcoholics; and her work with newcomers in meetings was legendary. They were her special focus. Her journal records every principle and concept that is part of the A.A. picture—Bible studies, prayer, Quiet Time, Guidance, Literature recommended, Oxford Group principles and practices, and practical guides to working with alcoholics. It seems likely that she not only shared the contents of this journal—written between 1933 and 1939—with Bill Wilson, but also that Bill took many of his Oxford Group and other expressions directly from Anne's Journal. If so, the fact has never been mentioned. It's fair to say that Anne Smith—if she ever becomes the subject of proper research, recognition, and approbation—will be seen as a real bridge between the Biblical Christian Fellowship program of Akron and the Oxford Group/Shoemaker ideas that were embodied in Wilson's Steps and Big Book. Anne saw and discussed both. See Dick B. *Anne Smith's Journal, 1933-1939; The Akron Genesis of Alcoholics Anonymous; A New Way Out; Twelve Steps for You.*

Example Number Twelve: The Devotionals and Christian Literature Read and Circulated. We know that A.A.'s basic ideas came from the Bible. The Book of James, Jesus's Sermon on the Mount, and 1 Corinthians 13 were frequently read aloud and studied and were considered absolutely essential. And AAs studied literature that discussed these roots—books on the Sermon by Oswald Chambers, Glenn Clark, Harry Emerson Fosdick, Emmet Fox, and E. Stanley Jones. Devotionals discussing concepts from the Book of James—*The Runner's Bible*, *The Upper Room*, *My Utmost for His Highest*, *Daily Strength for Daily Needs*. There were commentaries on 1 Corinthians 13 written by Henry Drummond and Toyohiko Kagawa and studied by pioneers. And various other concepts were fleshed out through the literature of Shoemaker on all aspects of the Bible, prayer, guidance, Quiet Time, and so on. So also through the many Oxford Group books on these subjects—*Soul Surgery* (and the Five C's), *Quiet Time*, *The Guidance of God, Realizing Religion*, *For Sinners Only*, *When Man Listens*, and so on. In addition, there were prayer guides, Bible study guides, and healing guides galore—in Dr. Bob's Library and circulated by him to others. The whole picture can be found in my titles: Dick B. *The Books Early AAs Read for Spiritual Growth, 7th edition; Making Known the Biblical History and Roots of A.A.; Anne Smith's Journal; The Akron Genesis of Alcoholics Anonymous; Dr. Bob and His Library.*

Example Number Thirteen: New Thought. Also beginning to take wing through the impetus of Christian Science and similar movements that flowered at almost the same period as the first two examples. But the New Thought focus was on a new kind of god—a higher power—that took descriptive words from the Bible but saw God, good, and evil in non-salvation terms. New Thought words and phrases like higher power, cosmic consciousness, fourth dimension, and Universal Mind filtered into the A.A. stream. The significant New Thought expositors included Mary Baker Eddy, Waldo Trine, William James, Emmanuel Movement writers, and Emmet Fox. See Dick B. *The Books Early AAs Read for Spiritual Growth, 7th ed.; When Early AAs Were Cured and Why; Dr. Bob and His Library; Good Morning: Quiet Time, Morning Watch, Meditation, and Early A.A.; God and Alcoholism.*

Example Number Fourteen: The Bible. There is scarcely a one of the foregoing thirteen examples that didn't involve the Bible in one way or another. I have written so much about the Bible and early A.A. that I want to do little more here than point to my titles which cover the subject like a blanket. See Dick B. *The Good Book and The Big Book: A.A.'s Roots in the Bible; The Good Book-Big Book Guidebook; Why Early A.A. Succeeded; When Early AAs Were Cured and Why; The Akron Genesis of Alcoholics Anonymous; Turning Point; God and Alcoholism; Cured; The Oxford Group and Alcoholics Anonymous; New Light on Alcoholism; By the Power of God; The Golden Text of A.A.; The First Nationwide A.A. History Conference; Twelve Steps for You; A New Way Out.*

Part 5

Look at Several Newly Researched Factors That Point Up the Major Structure of the Early A.A. Program

The First Factor is the Congregational Church

Bill Wilson and the Congregational Church: Most AAs and professionals have become so embedded in the "spiritual, but not religious" nonsense that they would shudder at any description of Bill Wilson's connection with Congregationalism. Yet Bill's family—both sides—were involved in the little, white, East Congregational Church that lies on the green with the Griffith family home on the north and the Wilson House on the south. We know now just how much was on Bill's religious platter as a youngster—largely dished out from his village's Congregational church. Bill's mother, Emily Griffith, was the daughter of Fayette and Ella Griffith.

Emily was in love with Gilman Wilson, who lived across the green. Gilly, as he was called, asked Fayette for Emily's hand in marriage; Fayette's consent was given, and in September of 1894, the two were married in the white Congregational church. The newlyweds lived in the parsonage. Bill remembered the time his mother was sitting at the piano and his father was singing a song about Jerusalem that climaxed with the word "Hosanna." Bill was moved by that song, was happy that Emily and Gilly were his father and mother, and that their music told him "of the Great Father whose arms are outstretched toward us all."

By several accounts, Emily's father, Bill's Grandpa Fayette, was a man of quiet faith, a reader, a Bible student, and a supporter of the church. Emily regarded that church as "her family's church." When

Bill's parents, Gilly and Emily, separated, Wilson, at age 10, went to live with the Griffiths and was raised by them through high school. From Grandpa Fayette and from his boyhood friend Mark Whalon, Bill Wilson developed an intense interest in reading. Mark gave him books. Bill borrowed books from a lending library, and Bill even read the big Griffith Dictionary. One biographer wrote, "The more Bill read, the more he wanted to read. He had read about Horatio Alger and Thomas Edison. He read *Heidi* and the family encyclopedia and, of course, the Bible."

There are some special points to mention about Bill's attendance at the Congregational Sunday School across the green. "All the Griffiths went to church," wrote one biographer. And the eleven-year old Bill Wilson went unquestioningly to the Congregational church. Over the years, Bill recalled hymns, songs, Bible verses, and temperance meetings from those days. But Bill's attendance was interrupted when The County Temperance Institute arranged for all the children in the East Dorset Sunday School to sign a temperance pledge. That did it for Bill. He stubbornly walked away from Sunday School and away from church, returning a few years later as he daily sat in chapel at Burr and Burton Academy while he was courting Bertha Bamford, daughter of a local minister at the East Zion Church. This too ended with the untimely death of Bertha, followed by some lean religious years for Bill except for his later marriage to Lois Burnham. The Burnhams were Swedenborgians. Lois's father was a Swedenborgian minister, and that family apparently inculcated in Bill many of the humanist and spiritualist ideas that later became a big part of his life as he and Lois held séances and engaged in other occult practices.

The Wilson family had an interesting tie to this church. The Articles of Constitution of the church were signed in 1838, and Bill's grandfather W. Wilson was one of the signators. There is a record of his contributing $22.50 to the church in 1839. In 1881 and 1882, W. Wilson was voted as a Collector at the church. And the church records show that Helen E. Wilson appeared on a list of members in 1890, 1905, and again in 1924. On January 9, 1913, Helen E. Wilson was one of the signers of the Articles of Association. Bill's parents were married there and lived in the parsonage. And it was Bill's Grandpa Willie Wilson who had been a drunk, gone to the top of nearby Mount Aeolus, and had a conversion experience there. This experience caused Willie to run down the mountain, seize the pulpit in the

Congregational Church, announce that he had been saved, and refrain from drinking for the rest of his life. Bill's mother apparently told that story many many times.

Consider the church affiliations from this viewpoint. The Griffiths lived on one side of the church, belonged to it, supported it, saw to it that Bill's mother was involved, and enrolled their grandson Bill in the Sunday school. The Wilsons lived on the other side of the church and seemed involved in its very founding, financial support, and administration. And the Grandpa Willie testimonial seems to show that the old gentleman felt comfortable unloading on the congregation service his salvation testimonial. Without further research, it would be hard to characterize Bill Wilson as a Congregationalist since so many histories paint him as "spiritual, but not religious," a "conservative atheist," and an "agnostic." However, these same writers have, for the most part, pointedly left Bill's childhood religious activities in total darkness.

But we now know that Bill's family—both sides, the Wilsons and the Griffiths—were involved in the little East Congregational Church in East Dorset, Vermont. Bill's parents were married there and lived in the parsonage. Bill attended Congregational Sunday school at that church. And it was Bill's paternal grandfather Willie Wilson who signed the Articles founding the church and later announced his conversion and cure of alcoholism to that same church. That's all I have learned thus far about Bill's Congregational Church connections as a youth. But it seems more than likely that, whether he was exposed to church polity through the Wilson family or through the Griffith family, Bill must have observed the Congregationalist traditions of the family church next door. And, like all Congregational churches, it was self-governing, self-supporting, and independent of any doctrinal rule from higher authority.

Dr. Bob and the Congregational Church: Dr. Bob's connection with Congregationalism was far deeper. Bob, his sister, and his parents regularly attended the North Congregational Church in St. Johnsbury, Vermont. Regularly meant at least four times a week for services, and prayer meetings. Bob's father, Judge Smith, was a Sunday School teacher there for forty years. Bob's mother was devoted to, and looked upon as a pillar of, that church. Bob specifically commented on his training and membership in Christian Endeavor—the young people's society which sprang from St. Johnsbury's North Congregational Church. And the original Christian Endeavor Societies themselves emerged from the Congregational traditions of New England. Again, it is fair to assume that Dr. Bob became quite conversant with Congregationalist polity during his exposure to it through his family's deep church involvement and through his own continued activity through the end of high school.

Autonomy in Groups; self-government; self-support; freedom from control; and the Congregational Church. This much should be said about the Congregational Church in view of early A.A.'s fierce group insistence on local group autonomy, local self-support, and local rules and votes by members, rather than "government" by "leaders." And nothing could have been made more clear as to that autonomy principle at A.A.'s beginnings than when Clarence Snyder broke off from the early Akron A.A. fellowship in May, 1939, formed a totally different group in Cleveland, was immediately voted out as Secretary in Cleveland, and then went on to help grow Cleveland A.A. groups from one to thirty in a year. Moreover, when Bill Wilson proposed the writing of a basic text for A.A., he felt obliged to go to Akron Number One for the vote, won the vote after a close and highly debated discussion, and then returned to New York to write a book that bore little resemblance to the very program which Akron had developed and authorized Bill to memorialize.

Definitions of Congregationalism: My internet research as to Congregational churches produced the following: "There are difficulties in identifying a specific beginning because Congregationalism is more easily identified as a movement than a single denomination, given its distinguishing commitment to the complete autonomy of the local congregation. . . . The early Congregationalists sought to separate themselves from the Anglican church in every possible way and even forwent having church buildings. They met in one another's homes for many years." (quoted from *Wikipedia,* and underlining A.A.'s "autonomy" Tradition).

The Second Factor is Conversion: Examined through the Salvation Army and the Rescue Missions

- ***Abstinence, salvation, Bible and Prayer, and compassionate work with others as the Salvation Army Influence.***

As far as I know, neither Bill Wilson nor Dr. Bob had any extended experience with the Salvation Army. Bill did, however, propose inserting in his will a provision that some Big Book and Wilson royalties go to the Salvation Army where it would indirectly benefit alcoholics (Letter from Henrietta Seiberling to her son John). Bill did grouse around the New York shadows and possibly visited rescue missions; but I've found nothing specifically identifying the work of any Salvationists with Bill. It would be no surprise if such evidence turned up in the future. One thing is certain: The AAs were very familiar with the Salvation Army story as rendered in Harold Begbie's *Twice-Born Men.*

On the other hand, the Salvation Army's work and ideas were widely known and had a tremendous impact on the religious recovery ideas being applied when A.A. was formed. Thus, when a drunk would stagger to the door of his home at Calvary House, Rev. Sam Shoemaker would often send him either to the Salvation Army or to the Calvary Rescue Mission.

Salvation Army religious principles and practices were known in the 1930's to be highly successful, long-standing, and very simple. The Salvationist history and program were memorialized in a huge biography of Salvation Army founder General William Booth by Harold Begbie and also in Begbie's *Twice-Born Men,* a popular book that was widely read by early AAs and Oxford Group people.

As summarized by a clergyman at the Yale Summer School Alcohol Studies Lectures where Bill Wilson spoke as well in 1945, the Salvationist program involved these five features: (1) Abstinence. (2) Reliance on the Creator and a relationship with Him through salvation by belief in Christ. (3) Elimination of sinful conduct and replacing it with life by Christian principles. (4) Growth spiritually through Bible study, prayer, worship, and fellowship with like-minded believers. (5) Intense work by one successful Salvationist with a newcomer outcast still suffering from drunkenness, criminal activities, and impoverished homelessness.

Each of these Salvation Army principles became a hallmark of early Akron A.A.'s basic ideas. And conversion leading to salvation was a foundation stone of the Salvation Army program and of the Akron "real surrenders."

- ***The special emphasis on "Soup, Soap, and Salvation" at Rescue Missions with their conversion messages about the power and gospel of Jesus Christ***

One can find doctrines about how a person is converted, becomes born again of God's spirit, and is saved. But the starting point should necessarily be the Bible itself which says:

> For God so loved the world, that he gave his only begotten Son, that whosoever believeth in him should not perish, but have everlasting life. For God sent not his Son into the world to condemn the world, but that the world through him might be saved (John 3:16 -17).
>
> That if thou shalt confess with thy mouth the Lord Jesus, and shalt believe in thine heart that God hath raised him from the dead, thou shalt be saved. For with the heart man believeth unto righteousness; and with the mouth confession is made unto salvation (Romans 10:9-10)
>
> Moreover, brethren, I declare unto you the gospel which I preached unto you, which also ye have received, and wherein ye stand; By which also you are saved, if ye keep in memory what I preached unto you, unless ye have believed in vain. For I delivered unto you first of all that which I also received, how that Christ died for our sins according to the scriptures; And that he was buried, and that he rose again the third day according to the scriptures (1 Corinthians 15:1-4).

The famous evangelist preacher Billy Sunday said as to conversion:

> What does converted mean? It means completely changed. Converted is not synonymous with reformed. Reforms are from without—conversion from within. Conversion is a complete surrender to Jesus. It's a willingness to do what he wants you to do. Unless you have made a complete surrender and are doing His will it will avail you nothing. . . . [William T. Ellis, *Billy*

Sunday: The Man and His Message (Chicago: Moody Press, 1959), p. 181]

Countless evangelists, healers, and clergy—many of whose books were studied by A.A. founders and early AAs—defined conversion in terms of the confession and belief spelled out in Romans 10:9-10 and quoted above.

> See: William T. Ellis, *Billy Sunday*, p. 181; R.W. Schambach. *Presents: God's Guarantee to Heal You,* Tyler, TX: Schambach Revivals, Inc., 1991, 110; E. W. Kenyon. *The Wonderful Name of Jesus*. Kenyon's Gospel Publishing Society, 1998, p. 31; Samuel M. Shoemaker, Jr., *If I Be Lifted Up*. NY: Fleming H. Revell, 1931, p. 83; Glenn Clark. *Touchdowns for the Lord*: *The Story of "Dad" A .J. Elliott*. MN: Macalester Park Publishing Company, 1947, pp. 55-56; T. L. Osborn and Daisy Osborn. *When Jesus Visited Our House*. OK:Osborn Foundation, 1980, pp. 28-29; Roberts Liardon. *John G. Lake: The Complete Collection of His Life Teachings*. OK: Albury Publishing, 1999, p. 473; F. F. Bosworth. *Christ the Healer*. MI: Fleming H. Revell, 1973, pp. 61, 140, 147-148; Victor C. Kitchen. *I Was a Pagan*. NY: Harper & Brothers, 1934, pp. 68, 79, 150, 176, 186.

Early AAs studied, heard, or visited the evangelists and the missions. And there is strong trace evidence that these sources implanted or reinforced some very important recovery ideas in early A.A.'s Akron program. These ideas were: (1) Abstinence. (2) Reliance on the Creator and coming to a relationship with Him through salvation by Christ. (3) Bible study and prayer. (4) An actual conversion service. (5) A stress on love, caring, and service to the outcast. These Christian Rescue Mission ideas and conversion records provided the foregoing basic approaches that impacted A.A.—particularly Akron A.A. Most of these ideas were specifically mentioned and then flatly rejected by Wilson and two companions just before the Big Book was published. The following are scanty accounts from several sources, illustrating just how many of A.A.'s messages from the Missions have been dumped:

Ever since his night at Towns, Bill had had no argument with God, and the impact of this sudden change had been far more profound than even he understood. . . . There were agnostics in the Tuesday-night group, and several hard-core atheists who objected to any mention of God. (Robert Thomsen, *Bill W.*, p. 255).

The conservatives, led by Fitz [John Henry Fitzhugh Mayo, a minister's son] who felt that since the movement was based on Christian doctrine, they should say so flat out (Thomsen, *Bill W.,* p. 282).

When the first members of AA were discussing the many possible names for their new book, Silkworth and Dr. Bob first supported the name "The James Club," based upon the principles of the Book of James in the Bible. During the writing of the Big Book, there were often heated discussions about using more Christian-specific language rather than the term Higher Power. . . . As badly as he initially wanted a Christian-based movement, Bill quickly realized he wanted other alcoholics to find sobriety much more; he realized the importance of this more generic Supreme Being to the value of an open-door invitation to the A.A. fellowship (Mitchel, *Silkworth*, p. 65)

Jimmy B. opposed the strong references to God, in both the steps and the rest of the early chapters. Hank wanted to soft-pedal them; but **Fitz insisted that the book should express Christian doctrines and use Biblical terms and expressions** (*Pass It On.*, p. 199, bold face added).

A few, led by our wonderful southern friend, Fitz M., wanted a fairly religious book **infused with some of the dogma we had picked up from the churches and missions which had tried to help us** (Bill W., *The Language of the Heart*, p. 200, bold face added).

Bill Wilson was no stranger to Gospel Missions or churches—certainly not Shoemaker's. In fact, whatever he did in his dark drinking days, it is also clear that his first stop on the road to recovery was at the very mission that was run by Rev. Sam Shoemaker's Calvary Church. Bill's "sponsor" and friend Ebby Thacher had previously gone to the Rescue Mission for help for his own alcoholism. Ebby answered the altar call, made a decision for Christ, and "got religion." Ebby was sober. And in addition to what he (Ebby) told Bill about the Oxford Group, about Christian principles, and about religion, Ebby made three points very very clear to Bill: (1) Ebby had overcome his drinking problem at the Calvary Rescue Mission. (2) Ebby had been converted there at the altar and "got religion." (3) Ebby could and did boldly announce to Bill that God had done for him what he could not do for himself—a statement quoted in the Big Book, and whose ideas were repeated there several times..

Bill lost no time making his way to Calvary Mission. He picked up a drunken fisherman as a companion on the way, believed he would go where there were "fishers of men," and staggered into the Mission for "soup" and "salvation." He said he wanted what Ebby had received there.

Bill then entered the actual mission services. There were hymns, Bible reading, prayers, and testimonials—followed by the "altar call." Bill went forward in the company of a mission helper, made his confession, prayed with his helper, and accepted Jesus Christ as his Lord and Saviour.

The documentation of this conversion is clear: (1) Mrs. Samuel M. Shoemaker was present, told me on the phone that she had been present, and that Bill had there made a decision for Christ. (2) It would be difficult, if not impossible, for anyone to claim otherwise since such affirmations were the heart of the salvation process at the Mission. The process is described in the writings of Sam Shoemaker himself, in those of his Assistant Minister John Potter Cuyler's *Calvary Church in Action,* and in the description in *The Breeze of the Spirit* by Rev. W. Irving Harris who was Shoemaker's assistant minister and was credited by Bill as one of the early influences on A.A. (3) Years later, in a talk she gave in Dallas, Texas, on June 29, 1973, Bill's wife Lois Wilson described Bill's Mission experience as follows: "Well, people got up and went to the altar and gave themselves to Christ. And the leader of the meeting asked if there was anybody that wanted to come up. And Bill started up. . . . And he went up to the front, and really, in very great sincerity, did hand over his life to Christ." (4) Bill returned home to Lois from the Mission, talked to Lois, and then left next morning and began drinking again. But he wrote in a letter I have personally saw at Stepping Stones, and in which Bill said, he had "got religion"—the very expression that Ebby had used and that Oxford Group people commonly used in connection with conversions. Furthermore, Bill twice wrote in manuscripts I have seen and copied from Stepping Stones, "For sure I was born again." [See *Bill W.: My First 40 Years* (Center City, MN: Hazelden, 2000), p. 147]

Bill's conversion at Calvary Mission had an enormous impact (seldom mentioned in the same company as talk about the Mission) on the A.A. program he later fashioned. Bill had heard from Ebby that Dr. Carl Jung had told Ebby's friend Rowland Hazard that there could be no cure without a conversion experience. Rowland affiliated with the Oxford Group in search of such an experience and, whether he had one or not, indoctrinated Ebby on the conversion concept and in the Oxford Group program details. Bill had himself known for years of his grandfather's conversion and cure in East Dorset. And, when Bill soon had his own "experience" at Towns Hospital, he studied the many accounts by William James in *The Varieties of Religious Experience* that told of conversions and cures at missions. Bill consulted with his doctor, who concluded Bill had undergone a conversion. Mitchel. *Silkworth*, pp. 49, 50, 51, 81, 100.

The Third Factor: Dr. William D. Silkworth's Biblical Influences on Bill Wilson and A.A.

Dr. Silkworth wrote the "Doctor's Opinion" in A.A.'s Big Book. And despite ever mounting evidence of his unusual Biblical influence on Bill Wilson, the good doctor's role has truly been short-changed by historians. In fact, were it not for a book by Wilson's friend Dr. Norman Vincent Peale and a recent biography of Silkworth by Dale Mitchel where the biographer did an in-depth inspection of Silkworth's writings and views, we'd know little if anything about Bill Wilson and his relationship with the "Great Physician" Jesus Christ.

Those who have called Jesus Christ the "Great Physician" have been using that language for centuries. Jesus even referred to himself as a physician (Matthew 9:11-12). And through the ages, he was repeatedly called the "Great Physician."

That Jesus Christ, the Great Physician, could cure Bill Wilson is a vital, recent, unique, and virtually unknown contribution to A.A. by Dr. William D. Silkworth. First, let's look at some things that Silkworth's biographer Dale Mitchel found and wrote in *Silkworth: The Little Doctor Who Loved Drunks* (Center City, MN: Hazelden, 2002):

> Silkworth's family remembers him as a deeply spiritual man, yet unsatisfied with any particular denomination. **A devout Christian, he** initially fit well into the temperance mind-set developing across the country. **For years he attended** a church that would also have an impact on the formation of Alcoholics Anonymous, the **Calvary Christian (Episcopal) Church**, pp.11-12 (bold face added).

Now let's turn to Mitchel's account of the many discussions between Dr. Silkworth and his patient, Bill Wilson:

> During his third visit to Towns Hospital, **Bill had a discussion with Dr. Silkworth on the subject of the "Great Physician."** Many theorists mistakenly believe this discussion occurred on his last and successful visit. In fact, Bill Wilson himself wrote that he had thought about this discussion **before he decided to check himself into Towns for the last time**, at the urging of his wife and his brother-in-law (Mitchell, *Silkworth*, p. 44, bold face added)
>
> The official AA position on Bill's experiences at Towns Hospital includes little mention of the amount of time he had already spent with Dr. Silkworth, particularly during his prior visit to Towns. Long before he had experienced his "enlightenment," Bill Wilson had grown to trust the compassion offered by Dr. Silkworth. They would spend hours talking in Dr. Silkworth's little office (Mitchel, *Silkworth*, pp. 44-45)

Bill himself wrote of the darkness that had descended upon him before his fourth and final hospitalization. Bill declared:

> "**But what of the Great Physician?** For a brief moment, I suppose, the last trace of my obstinacy was crushed out as the abyss yawned." *Bill W.: My First 40 Years* (Center City, MN: Hazelden, 2000, p. 145).

Later, according to Mitchel, **Bill Wilson wrote** in *Alcoholics Anonymous Comes of Age: A Brief History of A.A:*

> Alcoholism took longer to kill, but the result was the same. Yes, **if there was any Great Physician that could cure the alcohol sickness, I'd better find him at once." (**Mitchel, *Silkworth*, p. 44)

Bill also said that, just before he had his hot flash experience at Towns Hospital:

> I remember saying to myself, 'I'll do anything, anything at all. **If there be a Great Physician, I'll call on him.' Then, with neither faith nor hope I cried out**, 'If there be a God, let him show himself.' The effect was instant, electric. Suddenly my room blazed with an indescribably white light." (Wilson, *Bill W.,* p. 145)

Mitchell appears not to have known of Bill's thoughts and actions at Calvary Rescue Mission and with Ebby Thacher before, or possibly just after, Bill's discussions of the "Great Physician" with Silkworth during Bill's third hospitalization, and before his finally check-in at Towns Hospital. Yet that account by Bill himself strongly suggests Bill's willingness to seek help from Jesus Christ perhaps prior to *any* discussions he had on the subject with Silkworth.

Bill had met with Ebby Thacher and learned of Ebby's altar call at Shoemaker's Calvary Rescue Mission. Ebby told Bill that he (Ebby) had been to **Calvary Rescue Mission;** that he there had "found religion;" and that God had done for him what he could not do for himself. **Wilson himself then went to** the Rescue Mission, stated he wanted what Ebby had received there, and then went to the **altar and**

made a decision for Christ. As previously detailed, many years later, Lois Wilson stated in an address in Dallas, Texas, that Bill had there given his life to Christ.

And whether Bill was referring to his conversion at the Calvary Mission altar or to his hot-flash conversion experience at Towns Hospital not long thereafter, **Wilson twice wrote "For sure I'd been born again"** (Wilson., *Bill W.*, p. 147; Dick B., *Turning Point: A History of Early A.A.'s Spiritual Roots and Successes.* San Rafael, CA: Paradise Research Publications, 1997, pp. 94-98). I also personally found at Stepping Stones a letter by Bill stating that he [like Ebby] had "found religion."

As to Bill Wilson's subsequent conversion experience at Towns Hospital, Mitchel wrote:

> What is not known is on what day of this eleven-day stay at Towns Hospital the now famous "white light transformation" occurred. Most believe it occurred on the third day of his belladonna treatment and also after possible use of Phenobarbital. While lying in bed, suicidal, depressed, and hopeless, Wilson would accept anything to help him quit drinking. He had tried everything he knew. He had reached a bottom that he had never experienced. Just prior to his experience with "the veritable sea of living spirit" Wilson often later talked about, he chastised God and said to himself "I'll do anything at all. If there be a **Great Physician**, I'll call on him!" again referring to his prior discussions with Silkworth. Then, according to Wilson, he cried out, "If there be a God, let him show himself." . . . Suddenly the room lit up with a great white light. . . . All about me and through me there was a wonderful feeling of Presence, and I thought to myself, 'So this is the God of the preachers!' A great peace stole over me and I thought, 'No matter how wrong things seem to be, they are all right. Things are all right with God and His world.'" (Mitchel, *Silkworth*, p. 47).

The "Great Physician" Was, Of Course, Jesus Christ

In the days of Silkworth, Shoemaker, Bill Wilson, and Dr. Bob, there were a number of expressions which may not be familiar in usage within A.A. today. But in that period, when someone spoke of the Good Book, that person meant the Holy Bible. When someone spoke of the Great Physician, that person meant Jesus Christ. Here are just a few of the writings about the Jesus, the "Great Physician," that make this usage apparent:

> William Boardman, *The Great Physician (Jehovah Rophi).* Boston, MA: Willard Tract Repository, 1881; Ethel B. Willitts, *Healing in Jesus Name*. Crawfordsville, IN: published by the author, 1931 [a book owned, studied, and circulated by Dr. Bob in which Willitts repeatedly referred to Jesus as the Great Physician, pp. 66, 104, 151, 209, cf. 95]; Joe Mcintyre, *E. W. Kenyon and His Message of Faith*. Orlando, FL: Creation House, 1997, p. 79; T. L. Osborn, *Healing The Sick*. Tulsa, OK: Harrison House, Inc., 1992, pp. 18, 55; David Fedder. *Back to God: The Great Physician*, Oct.10, 1999, n.d.; F. F. Bosworth. *Christ the Healer.* MI: Fleming H. Revell, 1996, pp. 13, 83, 89; John Maillard, *Healing In The Name of Jesus; A Book of Devotion*. London: Hodder & Stoughton, 1936, pp. 24, 44; Canon B. H. Streeter and Lily Dougall. *God and the Struggle for Existence.* London: Student Christian Movement, 1919, p. 199; Elwood Worcester, D.D., Ph.D. and Samuel McComb, M.A., D.D., Worcester, McComb, Coriat. *Religion and Medicine*. New York: Moffat, Yard & Company, 1908, pp, 340, 342, 351, 363.

The Case of Dr. Silkworth's Referral of Another Patient to the "Great Physician"

Though wrong in attributing the talk to me, author Mitchel correctly reported the following:

> According to AA historian Dick B., in a conversation with Peale [Dr. Norman Vincent Peale] shortly before

> his death, Peale discussed the following account of a hopeless alcoholic named Charles. After Silkworth told Charles that his treatment was over and that, as a doctor, he had done everything he could, Silkworth told him there was an area in his brain about which he still held a reservation and that could be the cause of his return to drinking after he left the hospital. Mitchel, *Silkworth*, *supra*, p. 50. [My interview with Peale never involved the topic of the "Great Physician."]

Mitchel clearly refers to some of my own historical research of Norman Vincent Peale's *The Positive Power of Jesus Christ*. Then he says as to Silkworth, Peale, and Wilson:

> Over time, Silkworth and Norman Vincent Peale became very good friends. Dr. Silkworth and his wife once held their church membership at Marble Collegiate Church in New York where Peale was the lead pastor. Much later, during the Alcoholics Anonymous continued discussion on the validity of the Carl Jung theories on spiritual conversion, Peale held his stance in support of Dr. Carl Jung's belief that far too many men turn to physicians rather than to the minister for spiritual healing. Silkworth furthered this declaration in his own early writings, presented later in this book. A student of Sigmund Freud, Jung was instrumental in convincing Rowland H., Ebby's Oxford Group friend, and later, Bill Wilson of the importance of ego. An avid reader, Silkworth followed the principles of Jung and William James as they pertained to deflation at depth and the usual requirement of reaching a "bottom" to enable the alcoholic to first feel the despair of crisis, then accept the possibility of a Supreme Being as the answer. Silkworth referred to Jung in his speeches and saved a private letter from him. It was Carl Jung who impressed upon AA through his conversations with Rowland and Bill there existed an opportunity of a spiritual ("religious") conversion as a last chance for chronic alcoholics. Mitchel, *Silkworth*, *supra*, p. 51.

Mitchel's point about Silkworth's interest in a religious conversion of the type to which Carl Jung referred is particularly interesting when you compare it to Dr. Norman Vincent Peale's account of Dr. Silkworth and Charles K., a businessman in Virginia, who had become a full-fledged alcoholic; so much so that he had to have help, and fast, for his life was cracking up. Peale related the facts concerning Silkworth's patient Charles K. as follows:

> He [Charles K., the alcoholic] made an appointment with the late Dr. William Duncan Silkworth, one of the nation's greatest experts on alcoholism, who worked in a New York City hospital. Receiving Charles into his clinic as a patient, the doctor gave him treatment for some days, then called him into his office. "Charles," he said, "I have done everything that I can do for you. At this moment you are free of your trouble. But there is an area in your brain where you may hold a reservation and that could, in all likelihood, cause you to return to your drinking. I wish that I might reach this place in your consciousness, but alas, I do not have the skill." "But, doctor," exclaimed Charles, "you are the most skilled physician in this field. When I came to you it was to the greatest. If you cannot heal me, then who can possibly do so?"
>
> The doctor hesitated, then said thoughtfully, "There is another Doctor who can complete this healing, but he is very expensive." "That's all right," cried Charles. "I can get the money. I can pay his fees. I cannot go back home until I am healed. Who is this doctor and where is he?" "Oh, but this Physician is not at all moderate as to expense," persisted Dr. Silkworth. "He wants everything you've got. He wants you, all of you. Then He gives the healing. His price is your entire self." Then he added slowly and impressively, "His name is Jesus Christ and He keeps office in the New Testament and is available whenever you need Him." "I need Him now," said Charles softly, "right now, I need Him, and I will give Him myself." "Great," remarked the doctor." You will find healing and you will never need to come

back to me as a patient, only as a friend. God Bless you, and," he concluded, "He will do just that."

[Peale then tells how Charles came to Peale's church and found the doors locked. But, said Peale, Charles seemed to feel a Presence, a strong Presence in which was wondrous power and love. Peale then continues:] Reaching for his wallet, he drew out his business card. Taking out his pen, he wrote on the reverse side of the card, "Dear Dr. Jesus, this is Your unworthy servant Charles. Dr. Silkworth says that only You can completely heal me. I hereby now and with all my heart give myself to You. Please touch me in my brain and in my heart with your healing grace. I love You, dear Jesus." He signed it "Charles" and dropped the card in the mail slot."

"HEALING COMES. Charles stood quite still, unconscious of either rain or snow. Suddenly he sensed light and a pervasive warmth spread throughout his entire being, beginning at the head and running down to his feet. It was as if a great big hand touched his head in loving-kindness. He had the same feeling that a person has when after a long illness comes a sense of well-being. He knew for sure that he had been healed. There was no doubt of it at all. He felt clean with a cleanness never before experienced, and with it an awareness of newness. He had been reborn. He was a new man in Christ. Old things long held in his nature were passed away. We became acquainted through his card dropped in the church mail slot, and I met him later while on a speaking engagement in Virginia. . . . Charles never returned to his old life. He had many problems subsequently, but the power held firm. It never weakened. His healing, which came so dramatically, was permanent. He paid the full price, as the doctor had said he must. He gave himself, all of himself, with nothing held back; and he received the power, the full power, with none of it held back. See Norman Vincent Peale, *The Positive Power of Jesus Christ: Life-*

changing Adventures in Faith (Carmel, NY: Guideposts, 1980, pp. 60- 62.

Now Let's Return to the Original A.A. Program That Produced Cures

As stated before, the Frank Amos Report summarized the Akron program as follows:

- An alcoholic must realize that he is an alcoholic, incurable from a medical viewpoint, and that he must never drink anything with alcohol in it.
- He must surrender himself absolutely to God, realizing that in himself there is no hope.
- Not only must he want to stop drinking permanently, he must remove from his life other sins such as hatred, adultery, and others which frequently accompany alcoholism. Unless he will do this absolutely, Smith and his associates refuse to work with him.
- He must have devotions every morning–a "quiet time" of prayer and some reading from the Bible and other religious literature. Unless this is faithfully followed, there is grave danger of backsliding.
- He must be willing to help other alcoholics get straightened out. This throws up a protective barrier and strengthens his own willpower and convictions.
- It is important, but not vital, that he meet frequently with other reformed alcoholics and form both a social and a religious comradeship.
- Important, but not vital, that he attend some religious service at least once weekly.

There were Several Success Factors, Including the Foregoing Three, Whose Main Features Were Taken from the Bible, and Which Were Common to Early A.A., and to Its Contributing Roots

Remember that Bill Wilson has said many times that all of A.A.'s ideas were borrowed and that Dr. Bob had said the basic ideas were from the Good Book. So, it seems, were those factors which produced the successes among A.A.'s predecessors. These factors were:

- **Abstinence:** The real alcoholic must never, ever, drink again. See James 1:12-16.

- **Resisting temptation:** See James 4:7 – "Submit yourselves therefore to God. Resist the devil, and he will flee from you."

- **Conversion** (accepting Jesus Christ as Lord and Savior) to establish your standing as a child of God: See John 14:6 – "Jesus saith unto him, I am the way, the truth, and the life: no man cometh unto the Father, but by me."

- **Reliance on the Creator for wisdom, guidance, strength, healing, rescue, and forgiveness.** See, for example James 1:5 – "If any of you lack wisdom, let him ask of God, that giveth to all men liberally, and upbraideth not; and it shall be given him;" Philippians 4:13 – "I can do all things through Christ which strengtheneth me;" Acts 3:12 – ". . . Ye men of Israel, why marvel ye so earnestly on us, as though by our own power or holiness we made this man to walk? The God of Abraham, and of Isaac, and of Jacob, the God of or fathers, hath glorified his Son Jesus. . . And his name through faith in his name hath made this man strong, whom ye see and know; yea the faith which is by him hath given him this perfect soundness. . .;" Colossians 1:12-14 – "Giving thanks unto the Father. . . Who hath delivered us from the power of darkness, and hath translated us into the kingdom of his dear son. In whom we have redemption through his blood, even the forgiveness of sins."

- **Obeying God** – See James 2:8-10 – "If ye fulfill the royal law according to the scripture, Thou shalt love thy neighbor as thyself, ye do well. But if ye have respect to persons, ye commit sin, and are considered of the law as transgressors. For whosoever shall keep the whole law, and yet offend in one point, he is guilty of all.

- **Growing in fellowship with the Father through Bible study, prayer, revelation, study (Examples: 1 John 1:3-9; Acts**

17:11-12; James 5:16; 1 Corinthians 2:9-16; 2 Timothy 2:15).

- **Telling others the message,** helping them get well, and urging them to do likewise. See Matthew 11:4 – ". . . Go and shew John again those things which you do hear and see: The blind receive their sight, and the lame walk, the lepers are cleansed, and the deaf hear, the dead are raised up. . ."

- **Hanging out with like-minded believers in religious and social comradeship.** See 2 Corinthians 6:14 – "Be ye not unequally yoked together with unbelievers: for what fellowship hath righteousness with unrighteousness? And what communion hath light with darkness. And what concord hath Christ with Belial? Or what part hath he that believeth with an infidel?"

- **Taking advantage of Church, Bible fellowships, and opportunities for religious growth.**

Note that the factors common to Akron and its predecessors were not "Twelve Step" factors, but rather Christian practices Commanded by the Word and Giving Assurance of God's Favor

Put the foregoing together, and you have the principles that cured alcoholics before and at the time of Akron A.A. These were: (1) Abstaining from drinking. (2) Resisting temptation. (3) Converting to Jesus Christ. (4) Turning to the Creator for help, strength, and guidance. (5) Obeying the Creator by eliminating sin and living love. (6) Growing in fellowship through Bible study, prayer, revelation, and literature. (7) Witnessing through intense love and service work with others, bringing them to abstinence, conversion, reliance on God, obedience, growth in fellowship, and teaching them to do likewise.

Part 6

What Every Christian in Recovery Ought to Know Individually

All A.A.'s Ideas Were Borrowed, said Bill W.

Early in A.A.'s founding years, its co-founder Bill Wilson put the torch to the idea that A.A. sprang from just one source. He said frankly that nobody invented A.A. He said all its ideas were borrowed. And Dr. Bob broadened that picture by pointing out that all the basic ideas came from the Pioneers' study of and effort in the Bible.

The Failure to Provide Details Has Caused Too Much Self-Made Religion

Unfortunately, neither co-founder put in writing in one place all the well-springs that produced the recovery streams in Akron and New York A.A. Consequently commentators, both favorable to and critical of A.A., have had a field day with discussions of our roots. Most of them have a number of erroneous concepts so embedded in their historical approaches that they just never tell it like it is or like it was. Those who don't like the Bible say A.A. left it behind in Akron. Those who don't like the Oxford Group say it taught AAs more about what not to do than what to do. And those who don't like either the Bible or the Oxford Group have tried to quiet the waters by diverting the stream. They say A.A. is "spiritual, but not religious" even though any well-informed historian, scholar, clergyman, and semanticist would probably ask: "And what's the difference?" Nobody really knows, but the distinction without a difference leaves many in a sought after no man's land.

The real difference in how we characterize A.A. and all its sources is that, without a knowledge of A.A.'s various and diverse roots—mostly religious, people quickly make up their own sources. Their product is called "self-made religion." And A.A.'s co-founder Rev. Sam Shoemaker pointed out that this self-fabricated stuff leads to all kinds of nonsense—including "absurd names for God," "half-baked prayers," *and* "self-made religion," as Sam described the results.

So it is. Those who have spurned the religious origins and facts often say that our Creator can be a tree, a radiator, or a light bulb; or they might say that neither the Creator nor the tree/radiator/light bulb god is "Conference-approved." Some capitalize "Higher Power"—a sorry substitute phrase for the Creator—as if this universalized "power" is somehow sacred. Others write "higher power" in lower case—timidly offering it as something greater than yourself. They often go on to say that you really don't have to believe in anything at all. And many AAs respond in a predictable and badly confused way, by adopting meaningless phrases such as, "Don't analyze," or "Don't think and don't drink," or "Look for the similarities and discard the differences." Whatever these sagacious pieces of advice are supposed to suggest, if there is no other intelligent explanation, some in A.A. may add that the Big Book is A.A.'s basic text and let it go at that. "The Big Book says it, and that settles it" is a common A.A. expression. And that leaves us with what the Big Book says, but more of, and mostly about, what it doesn't say. And it is indisputable that the Big Book says very very little about A.A. history, roots, or early ideas.

The Suppression of A.A.'s Christian History Has Left the Christian Newcomer Bewildered and Awash

Some AAs today know that all specific mention of the Bible has been deleted from their basic text—even the deletion of those three "absolutely essential" parts such as the Book of James, the Sermon on the Mount, and 1 Corinthians 13. They can see Jesus Christ mentioned only once, and then as a man whose ideas are seldom followed. They've seen the Creator turned into a higher power which has often been converted into a radiator or a rock. At the same time, they hear about prayer and meditation and haven't the slightest bit of information as to what those ideas meant either in earliest A.A. or as used in the Big Book and Steps today.

Consequently, they are left with nonsense. Prayer to a rock? Prayer to a chair or a tree? Meditation on a radiator? Meditating while listening to Gertrude? Praying to what! Chanting to what! Listening to what—a light bulb? For assistance, their Big Book tells them there are "helpful books," but there is no longer mention of the Good Book which was the major source for their basic ideas.

Conflicting Histories Have Produced Conflicting Opinions

One of the greatest difficulties a new 12 Step person encounters is the variety of conflicting words and expressions found in the Big Book, the Twelve Steps, and Twelve Traditions, and the few A.A. writings by Bill Wilson and by A.A. World Services people in New York. Thus, the newcomer may hear that A.A. came from the Bible; and it did. But he'll see no direct references anywhere to the Bible, to chapters, or to verses. He may hear that A.A. got its ideas from the Oxford Group and then, in the next moment, hear that AAs left the Oxford Group, that Bill couldn't accept most of its ideas, and that it taught AAs more about what not to do, than what to do. This despite the fact that a careful study of the Big Book and Step language discloses that the language used was primarily that found in books and articles by Bill's spiritual mentor and Oxford Group leader, Rev. Sam Shoemaker, Jr.—whom Bill eventually called a "co-founder" of Alcoholics Anonymous. Then there are other curious anomalies: (1) There are clear Biblical descriptions of the Creator, such as Father, Father of lights, Maker, God of our fathers, Spirit, and others. (2) Yet there are puzzling, conflicting New Thought descriptions such as Universal Mind, Great Reality, and Infinite Love—all capitalized. (3) There are Bible phrases like "faith without works is dead," "Thy will be done," and "love thy neighbor as thyself" with no reference to their source, therefore often presented or discussed out of context with their Biblical meaning. (4) There is an absence of previously important Biblical words like "salvation," "conversion," and "remission" of sins. (5) Then the substitution of phrases like "ego-centricity," "spiritual awakening," "psychic change," and "God alone is the judge of our sex situation." (6) There is the explicit statement by each of A.A.'s founding members—Bill Wilson, Bob Smith, and Bill Dotson—that they had been cured of alcoholism. (7) Then Bill's insertion of the Peabody dogma, "There is no cure for alcoholism."

The Way Into the Heart and Mind of the Christian in A.A.

What to do with these conflicting meanings—learn their differences: The first approach to A.A. history is to learn that the A.A. program was not developed by just one person, that stories about its beginnings have been in total conflict, and that accuracy requires that it be described in terms of at least two entirely different programs. The original program came from Akron. The publicized and well-known program was fashioned four years later and published in 1939 by Wilson's Works Publishing Company—a profit oriented East Coast corporation.

The original program was developed exclusively in Akron under the leadership of Dr. Bob, partnering with Bill Wilson, Bob's wife, Henrietta Seiberling, and Mr. and Mrs. T. Henry Williams. All but Bill were self-proclaimed Christians. The New York Big Book program was assembled from contributions by atheists, Christians, New Thought writers, physicians, and a lay therapist—certainly not all Christians. Bill Wilson began his days in a Christian Sunday School, left it, later claimed he was a conservative atheist, still later made a decision for Christ at Calvary Rescue Mission, had a born-again conversion there or at Towns Hospital, and occasionally described himself as a "practicing Christian." (Bill so stated at the Yale Summer School Lectures in 1945).

Go for Akron if you want the scoop on Christian A.A.

In a moment, we will deal with the differing sources of A.A.'s two different programs. We will also point to their common ideas. And we will illustrate from their origins some major reasons for their differences.

The Akron Christian Fellowship Sources. (1) The first source was the King James Version of the Bible. How do we know? Dr. Bob said so on many occasions and particularly stressed the importance of the Book of James, the Sermon on the Mount, and 1 Corinthians 13. (2) The second source was the required confession of Jesus Christ as one's personal Lord and Saviour—done primarily in a small conversion meeting involving three or so "elders" and the newcomer. It followed the procedure of James 5:16 and meant surrender on one's knees, confession of Christ, a prayer to have alcohol taken out of one's life, and a prayer for strength and guidance to live according to the teachings of Christ, particularly those embodied in Absolute Honesty,

Absolute Purity, Absolute Unselfishness, and Absolute Love. The ceremony resembled those in the Rescue Missions. (3) The third source was the weekly "old fashioned prayer meeting"—very much like those in Dr. Bob's Congregational Church in Vermont. This prayer meeting was coupled with a Bible study segment, again following the lines of the church of Dr. Bob's youth. (4) The group was self-governing and self-supporting and met in private homes for several years—very much like the First Century Christians did and the Akron people did for some five years. (5) There was also a brief seeking of God's guidance in a "Quiet Time" circle—after the manner of Bob's Christian Endeavor, the YMCA, and the Oxford Group. (6) There was a discussion of topics—much as was done in Christian Endeavor. (7) There was recommended and outside reading—much as was done in Christian Endeavor and in the Oxford Group. (8) There was social and religious comradeship—common to most all the sources. (9) There was optional church attendance. (10) There was daily study of Christian devotionals like *The Upper Room* and *My Utmost for His Highest.* (11) There was daily quiet time by AAs and their families at the Smith Home each morning where Anne Smith would lead with a prayer, read from the Bible, have group prayer and seeking of guidance, read from her journal. and lead discussion of its ideas. (12) There was helpful counsel from Bob, Anne, Bill Wilson, Bill Dotson, and from others as they "graduated" and went out to form their own groups in Minnesota, Texas, Detroit, Cleveland, Little Rock, Chicago, and Indiana.

The New York/Wilson Sources: (1) The first East Coast source was Dr. Carl Gustav Jung, the famous Swiss psychiatrist. In the early 1930's, Jung informed his patient Rowland Hazard that Rowland had the mind of a chronic alcoholic and could probably not be cured without a *conversion* experience. (2) Rowland recovered through membership in A First Century Christian Fellowship known as the Oxford Group; and Rowland passed along to Ebby Thacher the Oxford Group principles involved in attaining what the Oxford Group called a *spiritual* experience—sometimes called "God consciousness" resulting from the alleged three-fold Oxford Group transformation from *sin* (the problem) to *Jesus Christ* (the cure) to a *miracle* (the result). (3) Ebby was lodged at Calvary Rescue Mission in New York, answered an altar call and made *a decision for Christ.* He concluded that he had been healed of alcoholism, and "got religion"—perhaps another word for "conversion" (which was a term rejected by the Oxford Group). (4)

Following the Oxford Group witnessing idea of carrying the conversion message to another, Ebby visited his alcoholic friend Bill Wilson, told him of the conversion, explained some Oxford Group principles, and roused Wilson himself to go to the Rescue Mission. There, Wilson answered the altar call, made a decision for Christ, and soon wrote that he too had "got religion" and had been *born again*. (5) Still drinking, Wilson decided to return to his physician at Towns Hospital—for a fourth time. The physician was William Duncan Silkworth, M.D., who had previously told Bill that Jesus Christ, *the "Great Physician," could cure Bill*—a message that Silkworth carried to other alcoholic patients on occasion. (6) Wilson there followed the advice of his friend Ebby, "humbly" offered himself to God "as Bill then understood Him," reflected that *if there were a Great Physician, he (Bill) should call on him for help*. Bill called out, "If there be a God, let Him show himself now." The room lit up, gave the impression of a blowing wind, and caused Bill to believe he had experienced the presence of God. As to which, Bill remarked, "So this is the God of the preachers." (7) Asking Dr. Silkworth if the doctor felt Bill was "crazy," *Silkworth informed Bill that he believed Bill had had a conversion experience* and had better hang on to it. (8) Bill began reading *The Varieties of Religious Experience* by the eminent Harvard professor William James. There James had recounted a large number of conversion experiences similar to Bill's, concluded they were valid, and *caused Bill to conclude that he too had attained a valid conversion experience* just like those described in the Missions and elsewhere.

The rudiments of Bill's recovery thinking were therefore in place in 1934: (1) Shoot for a conversion such as Carl Jung considered a foundational necessity and Bill had heard from Ebby Thacher via Rowland Hazard.. (2) Believe the conversion will occur in the same manner as it did in the Gospel Missions. (3) Stand on the William James's research. (4) Follow the Oxford Group principles that Rowland Hazard had practiced and taught to Ebby. (5) Start searching for others to receive witness—bearing in mind the Oxford Group slogan that "you have to give it away to keep it." (6) Concurrently, begin attending Oxford Group meetings in the company of his wife Lois and a couple of others. (7) Relentlessly seek out newcomers in Oxford Group meetings, in Towns Hospital, and in Shoemaker's Calvary Rescue Mission.

But Bill had no success at all in bringing sobriety to drunks he brought home, and very little success with those he met elsewhere. He said so frequently and so did his wife Lois. In fact, Bill honestly conceded that he had not been able to get one single drunk sober before he came to Akron. But neither historians nor Bill himself have been completely honest about the reasons Bill failed in his efforts to sober up drunks. The first reason is that Bill was a messenger without a message that could reach and stir the hearts of newcomers. Bill had not been a church go-er. He had not studied the Bible. He had apparently read little, if any, Oxford Group materials. And his youthful religious juggling had left him armed with the fact that he had been converted at Calvary Mission, had his hot flash Towns Hospital experience, and stayed sober; but disarmed by the fact that Bill knew little if anything about the Bible, church, or the spiritual reasons for his cure. History has it that Bill was told he needed to focus on the medical aspects of alcoholism and stop his "preaching." But what had Bill to offer either on medicine or, for that matter, on preaching subjects as to which he had little instruction and was unprepared. Vital to understanding Bill's inadequacy as a spiritual messenger is the knowledge of his own spiritual impediments in addition to other spiritual shortcomings, Bill had some obstructive special issues in his life—liquor, adultery, spiritualism, severe depressions, and later LSD experimentation—quite a big lump of spiritual problems to face for someone who was supposed to be talking about the Gospel and yet with no significant religious or Biblical training or Godly walk.

The Akron Crucible: The story of Bill's coming to Akron is itself a miracle. Upon arrival there for a business deal, Bill resisted temptation to drink by phoning for a drunk to help. Miraculously, he reached Henrietta Seiberling. I say miraculously, because she had already convened a prayer meeting to ask for Dr. Bob's recovery. See Dick B. *Henrietta B. Seiberling: Ohio's Lady with a Cause*. Henrietta arranged a meeting at her home between Bill and her friend Dr. Bob. And the two men experienced the touching of hearts that can so readily occur when one drunk talks honestly and freely with another still in his cups. The meeting lasted six hours. The two men hit it off famously. Shortly, Bill moved into the Smith home in Akron, lived there for three months, and then returned to New York—basically remaining out of touch with specifics in Akron. But the specifics were, as reported by Frank Amos, quite simple, quite well tested, and quite productive of cures. Bill did stay sober and in touch with some newcomers and Dr.

Bob. Returning to Akron two years later, Bill and the Smiths were amazed as they reviewed the Akron successes. And then decision to write a basic text telling the success story was shortly made.

My 17-year quest for details and documentation: Almost every historical item covered in this article was unavailable to me when I began my research. Piece by piece, book by book, I managed to pull the parts of our history together and to obtain the documentation for their accuracy. In order of search, I went to the books Dr. Bob and early AAs read. Next, to the journal of the entire program that Dr. Bob's wife Anne had written. Next to the principles and practices of the Oxford Group. Next, to how the whole Akron A.A. picture had played out. Then to the basics AAs had obtained from their study of the Bible. Then to the immense role of Rev. Sam Shoemaker in providing Bill with the specifics for the Big Book. Then to a study of the all-important daily quiet time of early AAs where, after becoming children of God, they studied the Bible, prayed together, sought revelation, and read scores of books. Now these historical works have been followed by many of my later books which have dealt with Clarence Snyder, God and Alcoholism, Cure, When Early AAs Were Cured, Why Early A.A. Succeeded, The Golden Text of A.A., utilizing the spiritual roots today, studying the role of United Christian Endeavor, applying the principles AAs learned from James, the Sermon on the Mount, and 1 Corinthians 13, forming Big Book/Bible study groups in A.A., using guide books for that work, Bill W.'s own conversion experiences, and the ways to end the bickering between AAs and religion and to focus on giving the child of God the true picture while he plods along the tortured path of intimidation, fear, bewilderment, and uncertainty he hears in meetings and reads in today's literature.

There's lots still to be learned and disseminated before we will have the entire picture of A.A. in focus. I had begun to realize that the whole Akron program was far more founded on Christian Endeavor principles and practices than on those of the Oxford Group. Piece by piece, other details emerged. There was the whole Shoemaker story and my discovery that the words in the Big Book and even the Steps were largely Shoemaker words and that Sam had been asked to write the Twelve Steps, but declined. More? Lots more research to be done. More on Carl Jung,. William James, Richard Peabody, William D. Silkworth, Henrietta Seiberling, Clarence Snyder. On Bill Wilson's manuscripts, on the Christian materials deleted from those manuscripts, on John Henry Fitzhugh Mayo who witnessed the shelving of A.A.'s Christian materials. More. More. More.

What we had in 1990 didn't add up to the whole picture, or even part of the picture. And the gap had left alkies to their own devices in fashioning substitutes. When Bill dumped the Oxford Group in the East, the Oxford Group details were omitted. When Bob and Anne died, the Bible in A.A. died with them. When Clarence Snyder got on the wrong side of Bill Wilson, the Snyder legacy disappeared until recently. When Henrietta Seiberling was put on the shelf, her loud reprimands to Bill Wilson about phony spirituality, séances, substitute psychology, and sick thinking were ignored, along with her futile protests. People began denying that Jung saw Rowland Hazard. Many just never even seemed to want to know about Anne Smith, the impact of the early A.A. books, the basic ideas from the Bible, the Sam Shoemaker story, or the devotionals.

Too much religion seemed to be the alleged fear. Yet not a peep about the inadequacy of too little truth. And repeated attempts to quash study of a program so obviously religious at its beginnings and so obviously religious today that one court after another has ruled that A.A. is religious, is a religion, and not explicable in terms of any "spirituality" detour.

The Refreshing Breezes of New Materials: There's a lot more to come. I've been able to field 29 published titles, 160 articles, 60 audio talks, seminars at the Wilson House, a talk "near" the Minneapolis convention, several large history conferences and cruises, and three websites where freedom of speech abounds and frequent visits have added up to over one million five hundred thousand these days. Others interested in history are finally beginning to let the cats out of the bags. Good stuff has just begun to come out about Dr. Silkworth. Good stuff has already come out about Clarence Snyder. Interesting facts are emerging from Lois Wilson sources. Some have dared to mention Bill Wilson's LSD experiments. Also his spiritualism sessions at Stepping Stones. Also his womanizing and the squabbles over his estate. Also his obsession with psychic phenomena, Niacin, and book sales. Also the deadening effect his years of severe depressions had on A.A. ideas and historical accuracy. And more.

For a long time, I felt the foregoing side trails in Bill's life didn't belong in the picture. They had to do with Bill rather than A.A., I thought. In fact, at Stepping Stones, I was asked to bypass their locked files on drugs and psychic matters; and I did. Yet I later found that others had trod that route and even published on it in A.A.'s own *Pass It On*. Then I discovered that a host of missing A.A. history materials, involving particularly Bill and Shoemaker, had been snatched from the Episcopal Archives in Texas and simply vanished—apparently trucked off by two A.A. admirers. And that was a real loss because several historians had tried to research them, couldn't find them, and were astonished at the gap. Some assumed they didn't exist. But they did and do, I believe. In fact, I'm almost certain I saw a pile of the Episcopal Archives papers while on one of my early trips to New York and before I had gone to Austin. And are these things part of the whole picture?

I certainly think so, but not the picture I'm primarily interested in. I was and am focused on helping the newcomer in our great A.A. Fellowship. I was and am focused on discovering every aspect of the recovery program that was used in Akron, and then in Cleveland, and then in the Big Book, and then by the host of writers who emerged during Bill's 1943-1955 depression period. But the Akron program of 1935 to 1938 is the one that belongs in the spotlight. It's what worked that counts. It's accuracy that counts. It's the complete picture that counts. And it's the relevance to our getting sober, getting well, getting delivered from the power of darkness, and loving and serving our Heavenly Father that count.

More and more history conferences, research, and panels need to be aimed at obtaining information, rather than perpetuating errors, omissions, and falsehoods. The why of it all concerns the need of the child of God who finds himself in A.A., who needs to know that the pioneers were all children of God, that what he hears today within A.A. and from religious sources is more likely to be erroneous than helpful. The child of God who is plagued with alcoholism and addiction today and finds himself in a Twelve Step program needs to have the spotlight turned on his needs. He needs to know it's OK to be a child of God. He needs to know that God takes care of His children. He needs to know the materials that prove that point. He needs to know he is not alone, not wrong, and not out of place. He needs to know the exact details about A.A.'s founders and founding and the successes that emanated from those people who were seemingly hopeless, medically incurable, and desperate to be relieved. He needs to know what they did, what he can do today, and what the expected results can be. In other words, if the pioneers had a 75% to 93% documented record of cures, so can he.

He certainly must find out for himself. Neither A.A. programs nor religious programs today are pointed at history or at teaching history to the newcomers. Within A.A., he may need to do lots of reading on his own. He may need to listen to speakers who talk about history. He may need to obtain a sponsor who wants to help God's kids and knows why that's important. He may need to join a study group that provides even more information. He may need to go to meetings where the emphasis is on God, the Bible, Jesus Christ, and victory. So too with conferences. So too with the people who are part of his religious, social, and recreational fellowship.

This book is about A New Way In to the heart and mind of the child of God who needs His Father's help and meets obstacle after obstacle to getting that help. It's the way which offers him unfettered freedom to access the facts, the Father, and the victorious life. And to do it on his own responsibility—in A.A., in church, and in his fellowship of friends.

END

Gloria Deo

Index

D

E

F

G

H

I

J

L

M

N

O

P

Q

R

S

T

U

W

About the Author

Dick B. writes books on the spiritual roots of Alcoholics Anonymous. They show how the basic and highly successful biblical ideas used by early AAs can be valuable tools for success in today's A.A. His research can also help the religious and recovery communities work more effectively with alcoholics, addicts, and others involved in Twelve Step programs.

The author is an active, recovered member of A.A.; a retired attorney; and a Bible student. He has sponsored more than one hundred men in their recovery from alcoholism. Consistent with A.A.'s traditions of anonymity, he uses the pseudonym "Dick B."

He has had twenty-eight titles published including: *Dr. Bob and His Library*; *Anne Smith's Journal, 1933-1939*; *The Oxford Group & Alcoholics Anonymous*; *The Akron Genesis of Alcoholics Anonymous*; *The Books Early AAs Read for Spiritual Growth*; *New Light on Alcoholism: God, Sam Shoemaker, and A.A.*; *Courage to Change* (with Bill Pittman); *Cured: Proven Help for Alcoholics and Addicts; The Good Book and The Big Book: A.A.'s Roots in the Bible*; *That Amazing Grace: The Role of Clarence and Grace S. in Alcoholics Anonymous*; *Good Morning!: Quiet Time, Morning Watch, Meditation, and Early A.A.*; *Turning Point: A History of Early A.A.'s Spiritual Roots and Successes, Hope!: The Story of Geraldine D., Alina Lodge & Recovery; Utilizing Early A.A.'s Spiritual Roots for Recovery Today; The Golden Text of A.A.; By the Power of God; God and Alcoholism; Making Known the Biblical History of A.A.; Why Early A.A. Succeeded*; *Comments of Dick B. at The First Nationwide A.A. History Conference; Henrietta Seiberling: Ohio's Lady with a Cause;* and *The James Club*. The books have been the subject of newspaper articles and reviews in *Library Journal, Bookstore Journal, The Living Church, Faith at Work, Sober Times, Episcopal Life, Recovery News, Ohioana Quarterly, The PHOENIX,* and *The Saint Louis University Theology Digest.* They are listed in the biographies of major addiction center, religion, and religious history sites. He has published over 150 articles on his subject, most posted on the internet.

Dick is the father of two sons (Ken and Don) and has two granddaughters. As a young man, he did a stint as a newspaper reporter. He attended the University of California, Berkeley, where he received his A.A. degree with Honorable Mention, majored in economics, and was elected to Phi Beta Kappa in his Junior year. In the United States Army, he was an Information-Education Specialist. He received his A.B. and J.D. degrees from Stanford University, and was Case Editor of the Stanford Law Review. Dick became interested in Bible study in his childhood Sunday School and was much inspired by his mother's almost daily study of Scripture. He joined, and was president of, a Community Church affiliated with the United Church of Christ. By 1972, he was studying the origins of the Bible and began traveling abroad in pursuit of that subject. In 1979, he became much involved in a Biblical research, teaching, and fellowship ministry. In his community life, he was president of a merchants' council, Chamber of Commerce, church retirement center, and homeowners' association. He served on a public district board and has held offices in a service club.

In 1986, he was felled by alcoholism, gave up his law practice, and began recovery as a member of the Fellowship of Alcoholics Anonymous. In 1990, his interest in A.A.'s Biblical/Christian roots was sparked by his attendance at A.A.'s International Convention in Seattle. He has traveled widely; researched at archives, and at public and seminary libraries; interviewed scholars, historians, clergy, A.A. "old-timers" and survivors; and participated in programs and conferences on A.A.'s roots.

The author is the owner of Good Book Publishing Company and has several works in progress. Much of his research and writing is done in collaboration with his older son, Ken, an ordained minister, who holds B.A., B.Th., and M.A. degrees. Ken has been a lecturer in New Testament Greek at a Bible college and a lecturer in Fundamentals of Oral Communication at San Francisco State University. Ken is a computer specialist and director of marketing and research in Hawaii ethanol projects.

Dick is a member of the American Historical Association, Research Society on Alcoholism, Alcohol and Drugs History Society, Organization of American Historians, The Association for Medical Education and Research in Substance Abuse, Coalition of Prison Evangelists, Christian Association for Psychological Studies, and International Substance Abuse and Addictions Coalition. He is available for conferences, panels, seminars, and interviews.

Good Book Publishing Company Order Form

(Use this form to order Dick B.'s titles on early A.A.'s roots and successes)

Qty.	Titles by Dick B.	Price
____	*A New Way In*	$19.95 ea. $ ______
____	*A New Way Out*	$19.95 ea. $ ______
____	*Anne Smith's Journal, 1933-1939*	$22.95 ea. $ ______
____	*By the Power of God: A Guide to Early A.A. Groups and Forming Similar Groups Today*	$23.95 ea. $ ______
____	*Cured! Proven Help for Alcoholics and Addicts*	$23.95 ea. $ ______
____	*Dr. Bob and His Library*	$22.95 ea. $ ______
____	*Dr. Bob of Alcoholics Anonymous*	$24.95 ea. $ ______
____	*God and Alcoholism*	$21.95 ea. $ ______
____	*Good Morning! Quiet Time, Morning Watch, Meditation, and Early A.A.*	$22.95 ea. $ ______
____	*Henrietta B. Seiberling*	$20.95 ea. $ ______
____	*Introduction to the Sources and Founding of A.A.*	$22.95 ea. $ ______
____	*Making Known the Biblical History and Roots of Alcoholics Anonymous*	$24.95 ea. $ ______
____	*New Light on Alcoholism: God, Sam Shoemaker, and A.A.*	$24.95 ea. $ ______
____	*Real Twelve Step Fellowship History*	$23.95 ea. $ ______
____	*That Amazing Grace: The Role of Clarence and Grace S. in Alcoholics Anonymous*	$22.95 ea. $ ______
____	*The Akron Genesis of Alcoholics Anonymous*	$23.95 ea. $ ______
____	*The Books Early AAs Read for Spiritual Growth*	$21.95 ea. $ ______
____	*The Conversion of Bill W.*	$23.95 ea. $ ______
____	*The First Nationwide A.A. History Conference*	$22.95 ea. $ ______
____	*The Golden Text of A.A.*	$20.95 ea. $ ______
____	*The Good Book and the Big Book: A.A.'s Roots in the Bible*	$23.95 ea. $ ______
____	*The Good Book-Big Book Guidebook*	$22.95 ea. $ ______
____	*The James Club and the Original A.A. Program's Absolute Essentials*	$23.95 ea. $ ______
____	*The Oxford Group and Alcoholics Anonymous*	$23.95 ea. $ ______
____	*Turning Point: A History of Early A.A.'s Spiritual Roots and Successes*	$29.95 ea. $ ______
____	*Twelve Steps for You*	$21.95 ea. $ ______
____	*Utilizing Early A.A.'s Spiritual Roots for Recovery Today*	$20.95 ea. $ ______
____	*When Early AAs Were Cured and Why*	$23.95 ea. $ ______
____	*Why Early A.A. Succeeded*	$23.95 ea. $ ______

(Order Form continued on the next page)

Good Book Publishing Company Order Form

(continued from the previous page)

Order Subtotal: $ ______

Shipping and Handling (S&H) **: $ ______

(** For Shipping and Handling, please add 10% of the Order Subtotal for U.S. orders or 15% of the Order Subtotal for international orders. The minimum U.S. S&H is $5.60. The minimum S&H for Canada and Mexico is US$ 9.95. The minimum S&H for other countries is US$ 11.95.)

Order Total: $ ______

Credit card: VISA MasterCard American Express Discover (circle one)

Account number: ________________________________ Exp.: ______

Name: ____________________________ (as it is on your credit card, if using one)

(Company: ____)

Address Line 1: ____

Address Line 2: ____

City: ________________________________ State/Prov.: __________

Zip/Postal Code: ____________ Country: ________________________

Signature: ______________________ Telephone: ________________

Email: ____

No returns accepted. Please mail this Order Form, along with your check or money order (if sending one), to: Dick B., c/o Good Book Publishing Company, PO Box 837, Kihei, HI 96753-0837. Please make your check or money order (if sending one) payable to "Dick B." in U.S. dollars drawn on a U.S. bank. If you have any questions, please phone: 1-808-874-4876 or send an email message to: dickb@dickb.com. Dick B.'s web site: www.DickB.com.

If you would like to purchase Dick B.'s entire 29-volume reference set on early A.A.'s roots and successes (and how those successes may be replicated today) at a substantial discount, please send Dick B. an email message or give him a call.

Paradise Research Publications, Inc.
PO Box 837
Kihei, HI 96753-0837
(808) 874-4876
Email: dickb@dickb.com
URL: http://www.dickb.com/index.shtml

Cover Design by American Creations of Maui

This Paradise Research Publications Edition is published by arrangement with Good Book Publishing Company, PO Box 837, Kihei, HI: 96753-0837

Note: All Bible verses quoted in this book, unless otherwise noted, are from the Authorized (or "King James") Version. The letters "KJV" are used when necessary to distinguish it from other versions.

Made in the USA
Charleston, SC
08 July 2010